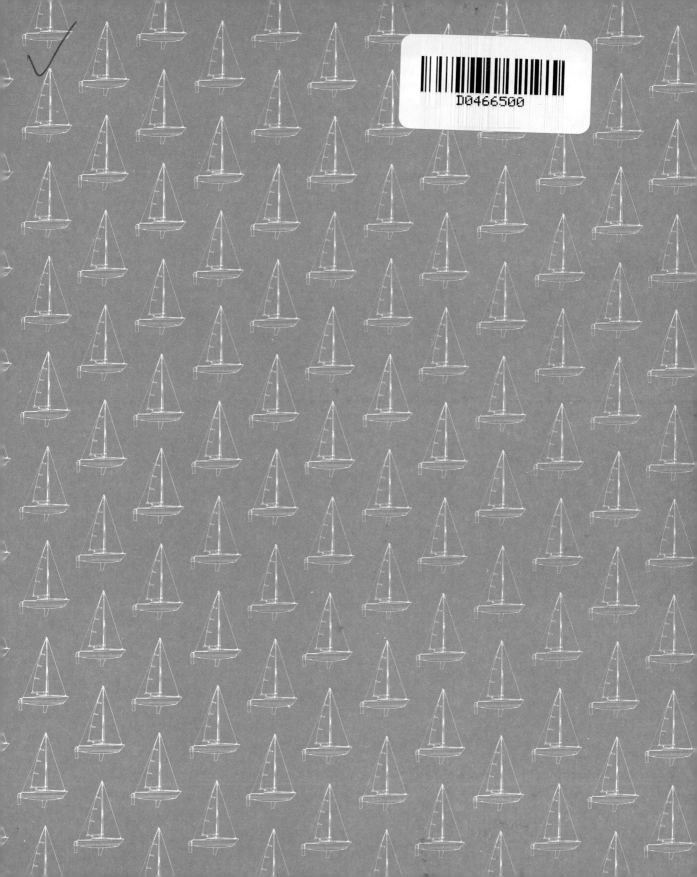

CRUISING BOAT
SAILING

CRUISING BOAT
SAILING

Bob Bond &
Steve Sleight

NEW YORK ALFRED A. KNOPF
1983

Cruising boat sailing was conceived, edited and designed by Dorling Kindersley Limited, 9 Henrietta Street, London, WC2E 8PS

Editor	Susan Berry
Art Editor	Bob Gordon
Designer	Julia Goodman
Managing Editor	Jackie Douglas
Art Director	Roger Bristow

THIS IS A BORZOI BOOK
PUBLISHED BY ALFRED A. KNOPF, INC.

All rights reserved under International and Pan-American Copyright Conventions. Published in the United States by Alfred A. Knopf, Inc., New York, and simultaneously in Canada by Random House of Canada Limited, Toronto. Distributed by Random House, Inc., New York. Published in Great Britain as *Cruiser Handling* by Pelham Books Ltd., London

First American Edition

ISBN: 0-394-52447-0

Library of Congress number: 82-48882

Printed in Italy by A. Mondadori, Verona

CONTENTS

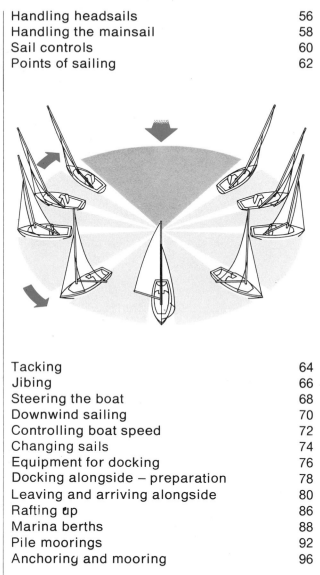

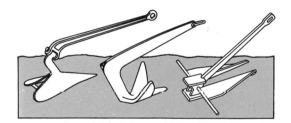

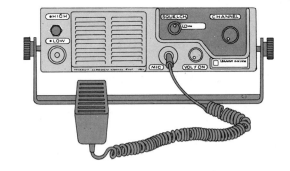

5482a

FOREWORD

Cruising attracts vast numbers of people of all ages, and at all levels of experience as sailors. Many of them have come to cruising boats for their first experience of sailing, while others have already acquired considerable knowledge on board boats or one designs. Some of them are inclined to think that there is not a lot to learn about cruising, encouraged by the recent developments in electronic navigation aids, and in streamlined, power-assisted deck equipment. It is, however, absolutely vital for anyone venturing offshore in a cruising boat to know exactly what they are doing, how the boat performs and how to cope with any emergency that may arise. They will, after all, be crossing busy shipping lanes, facing sudden and sometimes unpredictable changes in the weather and, increasingly these days, docking their boats in crowded and confined marinas.

We have tried in this book to use our considerable joint experience of sailing small cruising boats to make a clear, concentrated and readily understandable guide to the basic techniques of handling a small cruising boat. We have used a step-by-step course format, with plenty of photographs and illustrations to clarify the text, wherever possible. We hope that the book will not only provide a sound practical foundation for good seamanship for the novice skipper or crew, but will also provide a refresher course for anyone who feels that their methods have become a little outdated.

With an increasing number of families taking up cruising as a joint hobby, we hope that the book will appeal to both parents and offspring, encouraging them to get the maximum enjoyment out of cruising, as safely as possible.

Good cruising!

Bob Bond
Steve Sleight

THE DEVELOPMENT OF SAILING

Sailing is a rapidly growing sport with enthusiasts in most parts of the world. Its development as a sport, however, is relatively recent. What had formerly been the province, in the 18th and 19th centuries, of the rich alone was brought to the bulk of the population with the mass-production of fiberglass boats after the Second World War.

The sea has, of course, fascinated man for many thousands of years and from the very earliest times he found ways of turning it to his advantage. With considerable ingenuity, using whatever materials were to hand, he fashioned boats to suit his own needs and those of the local conditions. Rivers and lakes provided not only a rich source of food, but also the opportunity to move around from one place to another in a country which was often both thickly wooded and hostile. It is almost certain, therefore, that the very first boats were produced for use on inland rivers and waters rather than the open sea, since man had no knowledge of navigation, and the limitless expanse of the oceans was regarded with fear and awe.

These very early types of boat were probably simple logs which were propelled by the current. Gradually man began to lash these together to make rafts, paddled with a roughly shaped piece of wood. In areas where wood was not available, he used bundles of reeds instead, and reed boats of the same simple construction are still to be found today on the Nile and on Lake Titicaca, high up in the Andes in South America. With the advent of flints, man began to hollow out tree trunks to form dug-out canoes, powering them with wooden paddles. They are still to be found today in parts of Africa, in South America and in the Solomon Islands.

Sail power

By the time of the Bronze Age, ships were being made of planks nailed together, and the concept of the sail had been introduced. The first sailing boats are thought to be on the lines of the model ship discovered in a tomb in Egypt in 1906. Dating from 2400 BC, and rigged with a single square-sail mounted on a short central mast, the boat was steered by a large paddle-shaped oar strapped to the stern of the boat. The Egyptians retained this form of ship for some time, and the Egyptian square-sail rig spread eastward – it is still seen today around the waters of Malaya. The lateen sail was also, presumably, an Egyptian invention. A trapezoidal sail with a short luff, it was bent to a yard arm, set obliquely to the mast. The design was revolutionary in that it enabled the boat to sail towards the wind to some extent, as well as away from it. The precursor of the fore-and-aft rig adopted by most modern cruising boats, the lateen sail is still used today by Arabian dhows. A slightly different, squarer form, known as the lugsail, was developed by the Chinese. It consisted of a single sail, made up in sections,

Right, traditional rigs for working boats in different parts of the world. The Chinese lugsail, bottom, has been adapted for some modern cruising boats.

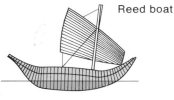
Reed boat

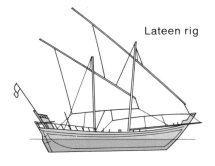
Lateen rig

Chinese lugsail

stiffened by bamboo battens and is also still in use, as the junk rig. Like the lateen, it is bent to a yard, but then slung to leeward of the mast when hoisted and set, with its tack forward of the mast. The lugsail is practical in that it can be easily handled and reefed.

To understand the design of modern sailing craft, it helps to know something of the development of the original hull constructions and types of rig, as many aspects of these ancient forms have been incorporated in modern designs. Then, as now, one of the main concerns of boat builders was for speed. Early boat builders realized that the efficiency of the sail was directly proportional to its size, and the larger the sail a boat could carry the faster it would travel. However, large sails were both unwieldy and uneconomical to use, except in parts of the world where labor was cheap. Boat builders, in the Western world in particular,

resolved the problem by splitting the canvas area into several smaller sails carried on more than one mast.

This square rig, with a beamy, sturdy hull and a high freeboard, was, for many centuries in Europe, the preferred boat design for large cargo boats. As new oceans were discovered and mapped they were built in ever-increasing numbers to take advantage of the new markets.

Around the coastlines of the northern countries of Europe, however, different considerations applied, and the variety of rigs which developed to meet specific local needs were numerous. Although the square-rigged ships, well suited to sailing downwind, could exploit the steady breezes of the trade winds, the craft plying coastal waters needed a more adaptable rig. A combination of the square rig with a fore-and-aft one (a modification of the lateen sail) was developed which allowed the boats to sail

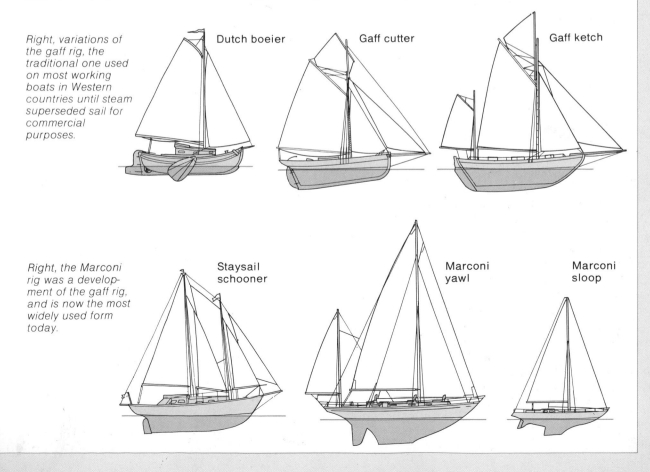

Right, variations of the gaff rig, the traditional one used on most working boats in Western countries until steam superseded sail for commercial purposes.

Dutch boeier   Gaff cutter   Gaff ketch

Right, the Marconi rig was a development of the gaff rig, and is now the most widely used form today.

Staysail schooner   Marconi yawl   Marconi sloop

well to windward. Barques and barquentines, brigs and brigantines, snows, schooners and ketches all plied the coastlines of Europes, each designed for a particular purpose – the type of cargo carried or the type of waters sailed in.

By the 19th century, the large cargo boats had been much modified and streamlined. Competition on the trade routes to the Far East and to Australia inspired the boat designers to find improved rigs to increase speed and efficiency. One of the most revolutionary was the clipper design originating in America, of which the *Rainbow*, built in 1845, was a prime example. "The vessel will never be built to beat her," declared the skipper. His confidence, although proved wrong some half a century later, was not surprising. The clippers could cut the sailing times of other vessels down by half. Their design was based on that of the Chesapeake working boats, with a very narrow bow, a streamlined hull and a combination of the fore-and-aft and square rig.

With the advent of the Industrial Revolution, the first experiments in powering ships with steam engines were carried out. These early vessels were unreliable and much scorned by the sailing masters, but, by the turn of the century, steam had overtaken sail for many of the large cargo and passenger boats, and in the years that followed only the small fishing and working boats still operated under sail power alone.

By the early part of the 20th century, engine power had virtually eclipsed the use of sail. However, people were beginning to turn to sailing for pleasure and recreation, and the now redundant sail-powered working boats were occasionally converted into cruising boats. Since those times the art of sailing has been kept alive by enthusiastic amateurs. Thanks to the increase in popularity of various forms of racing, boat design has been modified and improved to make boats not only safer and faster, but easier to handle. The double advantage of both adventure and a sense of freedom has spurred many thousands of people to take to small boats, and to cruising in particular, all over the world.

Left, the technology and seamanship required to handle racing boats like this one has, in turn, helped to improve the standard and safety of cruising.

Left, new rig developments, like these unstayed masts and wrap-around sails on the Freedom 40, have given cruising sailors an opportunity to sail with a minimum number of crew members, while providing efficient sailing.

Right, the cruising man's idea of paradise – warm waters and light trade winds in the West Indies.

The gentle art of cruising

Alongside the development of the large trading sailing ships had come the growth of interest in the use of small working boats as pleasure craft. One of the earliest cruising yachtsmen on record is the Honourable Roger North in the 17th century. His delight in cruising was little different from that of a contemporary cruising sailor: "I, with my friend Mr Chute, sat before the mast in the hatchway, with telescope and books, the magazine of provisions and a boy to make a fire and help broil, make tea, chocolate, etc. And thus, passing alternately from one entertainment to another, we sat out eight whole hours and scarce knew what time was past. For the day proved cool, the wind brisk, the air clear, and no inconvenience to molest us, nor formalities to tease us; so that we came nearer to perfection of life than I was ever sensible of us otherwise."

In the 17th century the term "yacht" had only recently come into being. Dr Johnson in his Dictionary defined it as "a small vessel carrying passengers". It derived from the Dutch *jacht*, the Dutch being the first yachtsmen, fitting out the narrow quarters of their small trading craft with touches of comfort, to use them for pleasure sailing as well as for work.

In the 1660s, Charles II of England was given a Dutch yacht, and became so enthusiastic about sailing that he ordered several small vessels to be built for him along similar lines. He raced one of them, the *Jamie* – a 25-tonner – from Greenwich to Gravesend against a similar small Dutch yacht owned by his brother, the Duke of York. The King, steering the boat himself, succeeded in winning the race and pocketing the wager of £100.

By 1720, the first yacht club had been founded – in Cork, Ireland – but it was not until a hundred years later that yachting became popular. The Yacht Club of Cowes founded

Below, Dutch boeiers from a 17th-century grisaille by Willem van de Velde.

Right, Jolie Brise, *winner of the first Fastnet race.*

in 1812, was to become the Royal Yacht Club eight years later, under the presidency of the Duke of Clarence. In 1844 the New York Yacht Club was founded, and the rivalry between the two clubs resulted in the founding of the America's Cup in 1820. This prestigious event probably did more to improve the design and performance of sailing yachts than anything else, as designers, boat-builders and yachtsmen fought to produce the best and fastest boat, with ever-improving technology and skill.

At the same time that yachting was growing in renown through the popularity of glamorous regattas, a small band of individuals eschewed competition and sailed simply to improve their mastery of a small boat in the open water. The first to leave any real record of his exploits was Richard Turrell McMullen. In the 1850s, when McMullen was sailing, yachting was still the province of the gentleman skipper, with a hired crew of professional sailors. McMullen set out to prove that a gentleman skipper could actually handle the boat himself. He learned his sailing the hard way – through experience – and said, "In this manner, getting into scrapes and out of them, I learned more of practical sailing in a few months than I should have learned in several years if I had a hired man to take the lead in everything."

McMullen did a great deal to prove that a small craft is no less safe and seaworthy than a large one, if properly handled; and he revealed the as-then unrecognized truth that it is the shore which is the danger for sailing craft, not the open sea.

McMullen died of a heart attack at the helm of his yacht, *Perseus*, in 1891 – just four years before another equally famous yachtsman, Captain Joshua Slocum, a Canadian, completed the first single-handed circumnavigation of the world in his boat, *Spray*. The idea of rounding the Horn in a boat less than 40ft in length was regarded at the time as suicidal. What made the achievement particularly spectacular was the fact that he sailed around the

Below left, a gunter sloop designed for coastal sailing; below, a Folkboat, a Scandinavian design.

Right, a classic gaff ketch – a traditional rig which is being readopted by some cruising boats.

world against the prevailing winds. In fact, the next circumnavigation in a small boat was not made for another 25 years and when it was, the route was via the Panama Canal, thus avoiding the rigours of the Southern Atlantic and Cape Horn in particular.

Much earlier, in 1880, the first cruising club had been formed in Britain, the object of which was to promote good seamanship, navigation and pilotage. Members were encouraged to explore the less-known coasts and harbors, and to produce pilot information on them which could be disseminated to other members. In 1902 the club received its royal warrant and appeared under the name by which it is now known, the Royal Cruising Club. Five years later, the Cruising Association was formed with the object of providing more information about harbors and ports, and encouraging safe and seamanlike cruising. The first book to be devoted entirely to the art of cruising – now regarded as a classic – was Claud Worth's *Yacht Cruising*, published in 1910. He explained the many branches of expertise which were required by the all-round seaman and handler of small craft.

After the early pioneering of McMullen, Worth and a few other English eccentrics, cruising grew rapidly in popularity throughout Europe and spread to the United States, where the Cruising Club of America was founded in 1922. Although the early cruising boats were all converted working boats, a Norwegian naval architect, Colin Archer, had turned his attention to designing craft specifically for cruising. A lifetime spent amongst the difficult sailing waters of Norway made him well qualified to produce sturdy, seaworthy boats. Erskine Childers, whose novel *The Riddle of the Sands* (published in 1903) gave literary expression to the art of cruising, commissioned Archer to design a successor to his boat, the *Dulcibella*, which had figured so prominently in the novel.

Although there was still a deep schism between the cruising and racing sailors in the early 20th century, the founding of the first public offshore race, the Fastnet, in 1925, did much to marry the two branches of the sport. The boats which took part in the first Fastnet

race were, in the main, converted working boats, like the winner *Jolie Brise*, a converted pilot boat. Unlike the boats of private racing events, such as the America's Cup, they were skippered and sailed by amateur yachtsmen. A new club came into being, the Royal Ocean Racing Club, and with it a new breed of boats, the cruiser-racers.

Modern advances in boat technology owe a great deal to the development of this form of racing, and, although there is still a great difference between sailors whose prime objective is to compete and those whose main purpose is to cruise, there is often less of a distinction between the types of boat.

Thanks to the new breed of boats, which are safe, speedy and easily maintained, cruising today, far from being the pastime of a few eccentrics, has become one of the most popular sailing activities. Competing with the elements, discovering new coastlines and getting away from the pressures of the industrial rat-race – these advantages have persuaded large numbers of people to try their hand at cruising. You can buy a boat suited to your need for pottering, or you can occasionally try your hand at racing. You are master of your own boat, reliant on your own skills for your safety, and you can travel where you will, at a speed determined by yourself, your boat and the elements. Small wonder, therefore, in an age where the individual has less and less control over his own destiny, that cruising has become one of the fastest growing sports around the world.

Right, a Rival 34 – a popular medium-sized cruising boat – exploring the coastline of the Isle of Skye in the Inner Hebrides.

BOAT CONSTRUCTION

For centuries the only common boat building material was wood, but there is now a wealth of different materials which can be used. Most mass-production boats are made of glass-reinforced plastics (fiberglass), a relatively recent innovation. In the period after the Second World War there was a changeover from natural to man-made materials, as the need for rapid construction methods became all important, in order to meet rising demand, and as the lessons learned in the development of the aircraft industry were absorbed by boat-builders. However, despite modern technological developments, there are still some boats being built of traditional materials and designs as many people prefer them.

The type of construction is a very important consideration if you are buying a boat, as some materials are more durable, or more easily repaired and maintained than others. However, the advice you are likely to get may well be biased, as each type has its own devotees.

Clinker and carvel

Clinker, or lapstrake, construction is the traditional form for wooden boats, and dates back to the Viking ships, if not earlier. It consists of planks of wood laid fore and aft, overlapping each other, over a framework of supporting timber ribs. Originally the planks were nailed together with wooden pegs, but later on copper rivets were used. The planks have to be thick enough to take the rivets, and, as a result, the boat is heavy. Clinker construction is not,

Traditional clinker construction is now mainly found on older working and dayboats (below right). The cross-section, right, shows how the planks are laid. Far right and below, a new clinker-built boat in the process of construction.

Cross-section of clinker-built hull

Copper rivets

Timber frame

Planking

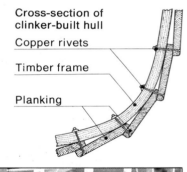

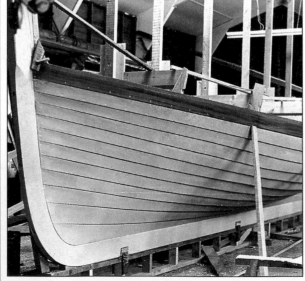

therefore, suitable for high-performance boats. Because of the weight of the boat, and the high labor costs involved, relatively few are built today, although you will usually find a number of clinker-built boats on the second-hand market, as they are sturdy and last well.

Another traditional form of wooden construction is the carvel method. Using a similar system of supporting ribs and frames, the planks are of solid timber, laid fore and aft over the ribs, but flush with each other, rather than overlapping. The planks are bevelled off slightly at the edges to produce a V-shaped groove into which a form of flexible filler, known as caulking, (traditionally strands of cotton soaked in pitch) is forced between the joints to make them watertight. The final finish is smooth, and the boat itself is sturdy and durable, like the clinker boat, and nearly as heavy.

Plywood construction

The development of plywood revolutionized the wooden boat-building industry, as its construction – thin strips of wood with the grains running in different directions and glued together – produces a stronger but much lighter material than solid wood. In marine plywood, a waterproof glue is used.

Plywood is very popular with amateur boatbuilders, but has the drawback that it can only be bent in one direction at a time, so that if it is bent along its length to form a curve to the hull, fore-and-aft, it cannot also be bent across its width to give a rounded side to the boat. This limitation has produced a form of construction known as chine, where the pieces of plywood are laid in sections, with two or three major angles, to form the shaped side to the hull. Single chine construction gives a rather hard,

Carvel construction is similar to clinker and new boats are quite rare. The cross-section, right, shows the flush planks. Far right, a typical double-ended small work boat; below, a cruiser being refitted and, below right, a traditional dayboat.

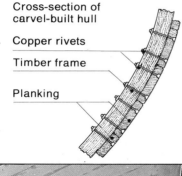

Cross-section of carvel-built hull

Copper rivets

Timber frame

Planking

unattractive edge to the sides of the boat, but it is simple and cheap to build. A more sophisticated form, known as double- or multi-chine, can be used, in which the pieces of ply are cut in narrower strips to allow the side edges to have a more rounded shape.

Plywood can also be used to make a modified form of clinker construction. Planks of ply are used, their overlapping edges joined with watertight glues, to produce a simulated clinker form, and thus a rounded hull shape.

The early designs for plywood boats followed the traditional building methods, and the boats were constructed upside-down on wooden frames. The stem, transom, keel and chines were erected first, before the boat was planked up with plywood.

Nowadays, various systems of construction have been developed to allow speedy building – often with the boat being built the right way up, and worked on from the inside first. Little framing is required since the interior construction, the bunks for example, provide the stiffening for the hull.

Although plywood cannot be bent in more than one direction, another form of plywood construction – molded wood – can. It uses veneers laid over a mold, with the grain of each layer running in a different direction to the previous one. The veneers are bonded together with resin glue, to produce a light, strong and completely watertight hull. Since the method of construction incorporates a mold, and needs skilled labor to produce it, it is relatively expensive, and is, therefore, mostly used for high-performance racing boats.

Fiberglass construction

Today, more boats are built out of fiberglass than any other material. It is the only method of boat building in which the material for the hull is created as the hull is actually shaped. An exact prototype of the boat to be constructed is created in traditional materials and a female mold is then cast from it, usually using the same techniques that are later used for the actual boat. Since the mold takes some time to produce, and has to be perfect, the cost of this construction is high, unless it is offset by

Above, a GRP deck moulding being lowered onto the hull. Below, once the join is made and cleaned off, a rubbing strip is added for reinforcement.

producing a number of boats from one mold. The mold is first prepared by waxing and polishing to get it completely smooth, and is then coated with a releasing agent which allows the finished boat to be removed easily from the mold. A gel-coat resin is brushed over the surface of the mold to form the outer surface of the hull. Layers of fiberglass are then laid inside the mold, brushed or rollered with resin as they are laid. Subsequent layers of fiberglass and resin are built up until the hull is of the required thickness. The resin sets hard, producing a hull form duplicating that of the mold. Once the material has cured, it can be lifted out of the mold, which is re-used for the next boat. Decks and interior parts can be molded in the same way and added to the hull, or wooden decks and fittings can be attached to the hull. The material, on the whole, is easy to maintain and, being constructed in one piece, is leakproof. Although they are relatively cheap to buy, the boats can look rather like bath-tubs! However, fiberglass can be used to produce the rounded forms that plywood cannot, and, in fact, gains in strength by having a number of curves in the hull shape.

Ferrocement

Ferrocement was first used as a boat-building material in the mid-nineteenth century, and was quite widely used for ship construction in the First and Second World Wars. It was not until relatively recently, however, that the techniques for building ferro-boats were properly understood, and even now many boats are badly constructed, because amateur boat-builders have run away with the idea that little expertise or skill is needed to put a ferro hull together. However, provided the boat has been properly designed and constructed, it can be extremely durable and cheap to maintain and repair. Although the material is relatively heavy, it is well-suited to larger cruising boats and commercial craft, and, in fact, can be molded into attractive shapes as easily, if not more easily, than some forms of wood construction.

The construction usually starts with a hull skeleton put together using layers of steel rods, laid at right angles to each other, and subsequently covered with wire mesh, which is then plastered over with a strong cement mortar, inside and out. The resulting structure is leakproof, impervious to corrosion, fire and rot.

Left, the initial structure of a ferrocement boat comprises a steel framework connected by steel rod stringers. Layers of wire mesh are laid over the framework and held in place by wire ties. When the reinforcing is complete the hull can be plastered.

CLOTHING

You can usually distinguish an experienced cruising sailor from a novice by the way he dresses — he pays more attention to comfort than to appearance! If you are sailing in cold climates, or in rough weather, you should take care to wear clothing which will keep you warm and dry.

In temperate climates, you will need two layers of clothing: an under layer to keep you warm and an outer layer to keep you dry. If you buy the cellular clothing now available, you will find it both practical and efficient. The fleecy pile traps the air next to your skin and helps to keep you warm. Because you usually only need one layer, movement is not so restricted as it would be with several layers of ordinary clothing. Cellular clothing also takes up much less stowage space. Several layers of thin, warm, ordinary woollen clothing will serve the same purpose; remember that two thin sweaters are warmer than one thick one, because the air trapped between the layers acts as insulation.

For the outer layer you must buy good-quality waterproof gear — don't skimp when buying it as you need the best you can afford.

There is a wide range of waterproof clothing on the market these days. You can opt for almost any type, from lightweight smocks and over-trousers to one-piece suits and heavy-duty two-piece suits with chest-high trousers. Most people who sail in temperate climates prefer the latter since they are strong enough and sufficiently waterproof to stand up to bad weather; the trousers can be worn without the top in better weather.

Since space is at a premium on board, try to take the minimum of clothing with you. You must, of course, have at least one change of clothing. Put anything you may need in a hurry into a small plastic bag inside your sailing bag. You will probably need a sleeping bag, preferably a tapered one with a quick-drying filling. If you are a visiting crew member, check with your skipper what you need to take. Once aboard, if you wish to be invited back, keep your gear stowed neatly in one place.

Sailing bag

If you are cruising for the first time, don't come aboard with your possessions in a couple of rigid suitcases — you will make yourself very unpopular with the skipper. There is very little stowage room on board most cruisers, so pack your possessions into a lightweight, waterproof bag, preferably of the type shown below, with stout handles and a strong zipper. Two small bags may be better than one large one; you can put your sailing gear in one, and your personal things in the other.

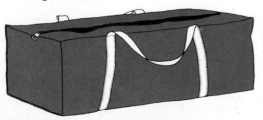

Footwear

Your footwear forms a vital part of your safety equipment. You must have shoes or boots with flat rubber soles and with an indented pattern which grips well on wet, slippery decks. Deck shoes are best for hot weather, boots for cold and wet weather. Buy the boots a size larger than normal so you can wear thick socks inside.

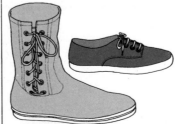

Tread contact areas

Good

Bad

Tread pattern
You need a tread pattern with deep wide grooves and as many edges as possible to give you a really good grip on the decking.

Good

Bad

Waterproof suits

A heavy-duty waterproof suit with chest-high trousers and a front-fastening jacket is the most popular form of protection for coastal cruising. The best types are made of strong, durable PVC or tough woven nylon with a nylon or neoprene lining to prevent excessive condensation.

Chest-high trousers

Jacket with hood

Double-fold gusset

The skipper is wearing a two-piece suit, with a nylon lining. Some suits have a safety harness incorporated: the advantage is that the harness is ready whenever needed, and will probably be used, the disadvantage that the suit may wear out before the harness does. For details of safety equipment, see pages 24–25.

Waterproofing

Your sailing clothing must have two essential qualities – it must be windproof and waterproof. Modern waterproof clothing is made of lightweight cloth with bonded seams to prevent leaks. You will find cruising acutely uncomfortable if your clothing allows water to seep through flaps and openings, so buy the best quality available, and mend any tears carefully.

Doubled flaps help prevent water seeping through openings.

Elasticated storm cuffs stop water from running up your sleeves.

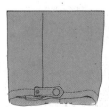

Special clip fastenings on trousers help to keep water out.

SAFETY EQUIPMENT

You must have a lifejacket and safety harness aboard the boat for each crew member. Although small boat sailors often prefer buoyancy aids, on a cruiser you need a lifejacket which will support you completely. There are various types to choose from, but most people prefer the kind that are worn deflated, since they are less cumbersome than those with in-built buoyancy. Most types on the market can be inflated either by a quick-release CO_2 cylinder, or by mouth.

Before setting out on a cruise, every crew member should be given a safety harness, which they should adjust to their own body size. Each harness should then be marked, so that a crew member can recognize his or her own immediately, and it should be kept where it can be reached easily when needed.

In freshening winds or when sailing at night, all crew members should wear their harnesses, and should clip on the lifelines if they are working on deck. Inexperienced crew members should be warned of likely dangers – the boom crashing across the boat, or unexpected heeling caused by an unplanned jibe or a broach. All boots and shoes worn on deck should have flat rubber soles with a good tread pattern, to give as much grip as possible on a wet and slippery deck. Obstructions likely to cause an accident should be kept to a minimum, and all equipment should be securely tied down, with no loose ends lying on deck.

Lifejackets

Many people argue that lifejackets are superfluous on a cruising boat if the emphasis is placed on staying on board, using proper safety precautions and a safety harness whenever necessary. However, every cruising boat must have enough lifejackets on board, of the right size and type for every crew member, and they should be regularly serviced and checked. There are times when everyone, regardless of experience, should wear a lifejacket – in a tender, in fog (when a safety harness should not be used in case the boat is in a collision) and in very bad weather. Non-swimmers, nervous beginners and children should be made to wear lifejackets, even when the boat is in harbor.

There are many types of lifejacket for general cruising, but the most suitable kind for cruising is the one that is inflated automatically by a gas cylinder, or blown up by mouth, and which carries enough buoyancy when inflated to float a full-grown man in the water, turned over onto his back. The types with no in-built buoyancy are less bulky and very comfortable to wear, but are not really suitable for non-swimmers or children, who should wear ones with partial buoyancy, the remainder of which is provided if needed, by pulling a rip-cord to a gas cylinder. Since there is a danger if you go overboard that your jacket may come off over your head, buy the type which has an additional strap from the back of the neck to the waistband, and make sure it is properly fastened, tightly enough to keep it in position when you are in the water.

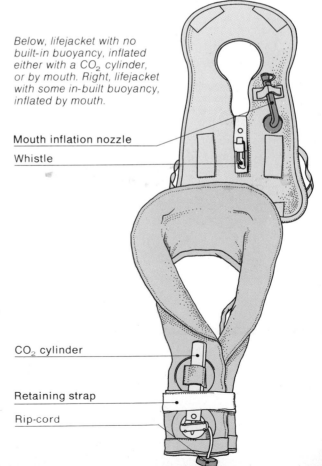

Below, lifejacket with no built-in buoyancy, inflated either with a CO_2 cylinder, or by mouth. Right, lifejacket with some in-built buoyancy, inflated by mouth.

Mouth inflation nozzle

Whistle

CO_2 cylinder

Retaining strap

Rip-cord

Combined jacket and harness

One of the best safety aids recently on the market is the combined harness and lifejacket. This purpose-designed garment provides a solution to the argument about whether a lifejacket or safety harness should be worn. The lifejacket of the combined model is worn deflated and then inflated either automatically or by mouth if needed. The garment incorporates back and crotch straps to prevent it riding up when in the water. The lifeline can be detached from the harness so the garment can be used as a lifejacket alone.

The combined safety harness and lifejacket.

The combined harness and jacket correctly fitted.

Safety harnesses

The safety harness is designed to keep the wearer secured to the boat by means of a lifeline, so that he is free to use both hands to work. The lifeline should have a quick release clip at both ends, so that if the wearer finds himself in difficulty he can free himself rapidly. Normally, the end of the lifeline is attached to a deck eye or to wire or rope jackstays which are rigged along each side deck. Your safety harness and lifeline must be of approved manufacture. The Fastnet race in 1979 made it quite clear that some safety harness clips were inadequate – they simply buckled and opened up under pressure. Because people are often lazy about putting on a harness, manufacturers have produced a waterproof suit with a harness incorporated into the jacket. Although the suit may well wear out before the harness does, it has the advantage that the harness is always at hand.

Left, crew member working on the foredeck, wearing a safety harness, and with the lifeline clipped to the jackstay.

Standard safety harness with lifeline attached. The line must have stout quick-release buckles at either end, and should be approximately 2m (6ft) long, of nylon rope or webbing.

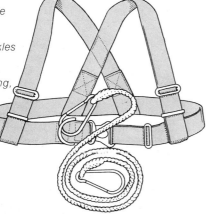

Fastening the lifeline to the harness

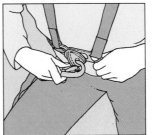

1 *Push back the clip fastening on the lifeline and insert the hook of the harness.*

2 *Release the clip fastening to lock the lifeline onto the harness fitting.*

STARTING TO CRUISE

Cruising offers much more scope than small boat sailing, and appeals to a broader range of people, young and old. It is particularly well suited for a family that enjoys being out in the fresh air, and wants to spend time together doing something in which all the members can all play an active part. Much of your enjoyment of the sport will depend on picking the right sort of boat, and although the information on pages 32–3 gives you some idea of what is available, you should seek a broad spectrum of specialist advice before committing yourself, and your cash, to a particular boat.

A large number of people come to sailing cruisers when the rigors of small boat sailing no longer appeal. Although they understand the basic concepts of sailing, they find that they have quite a lot to learn about handling a bigger boat. There is a great deal of complex equipment, especially now that vast strides are being made in marine technology, and the responsibility of handling a large boat in crowded waters, with a crew of several people on board, is not one to be undertaken lightly.

Certificates are becoming increasingly necessary to take any kind of vessel out on open water. Although this doesn't apply to every country, there is a growing need for all skippers of cruising boats to have gained wide enough experience to be certain of handling their boats properly in emergencies, at night, in bad weather and in congested waters. Anyone who cruises regularly is probably going to cover quite long distances, perhaps cruising in foreign waters at some point. They will be sailing in and out of major shipping lanes, sometimes in bad weather, or in poor visibility. They must know the international rules and regulations, and they must be well-versed in the techniques of safe and efficient seamanship; they must also have at least one person on board with a thorough grounding in the rules of navigation. It is not, in fact, within the scope of this book to teach navigation. However the skipper of any boat must have taken a navigation course, or have had sufficient practical experience under a competent navigator to know how to work out a passage plan, take bearings, fix a position, check tidal flow, and know how to use charts and pilot books (see also pages 128–9).

There is a wide range of practical navigation books on the market, and many evening classes and courses; proficiency, both theoretical and practical, is vital to the safety of both boat and crew.

A willing crew, coming to bigger boats from day sailers, should find plenty of opportunities to sail: useful efficient and practical crew members are sought after. Yacht clubs and magazine advertisements will direct you to skippers seeking a crew. Never pretend you know more than you do, and if you want to gain experience, take a sailing course at a recognized school, and add a few certificates to your actual sailing hours logged. Even the experienced crew member or skipper will find it worthwhile to go back from time to time for refresher courses to brush up on techniques, and to improve his or her skills.

This book is aimed at the relatively inexperienced sailor who wants to learn how to skipper or crew a boat efficiently, limiting themselves to fairly gentle coastal cruising. However, provided that the boat you sail in is seaworthy, you should be able to venture farther afield as you gain experience.

Before setting out on a cruise, the skipper must be well-versed in both practical and navigational skills.

PLANNING A CRUISE

If you are skippering a boat, the enjoyment you get out of your sailing will be directly related to your ability to plan your cruising with care, forethought and common sense. In your first sailing season, if you are a novice boat skipper, you will probably begin by making day trips; then, as you gain experience and confidence, you may venture farther afield.

One of the prime considerations when planning a cruise is the size of your crew and its suitability for your boat. When day-sailing, this is not particularly important, but as soon as you begin to undertake longer voyages, you must think very carefully about the composition of your crew. Some of them must be experienced enough to stand in for you as skipper, particularly if you are sailing at night, and you must be able to rely on them to carry out your instructions properly, and to use their initiative when necessary.

Always make sure that an unfamiliar crew is properly briefed: that they know what clothing to bring, what safety equipment you have on board and what your passage plan is. Take care when making a passage plan that you do not demand too much from an inexperienced crew. You must explain before setting off how all the equipment works, and, once sailing, what you want them to do, in non-nautical language if necessary, without treating them as though they were idiots! If they make mistakes, try hard not to hurl abuse at them. You will only sap their confidence and more errors will occur. If you do lose your temper, apologize afterwards and explain why it was so important that they followed your instructions carefully.

If you happen to be the inexperienced crew member, or even a more experienced one, remember that there is only room for one skipper on board. Don't contradict the skipper or argue about methods unless you have an excellent reason. If you really think the skipper is endangering your life, say so and ask to be put ashore!

As far as the boat is concerned, it must be seaworthy, clean and in good working order. All the equipment should be checked before sailing and there should be adequate spares on board, as well as all the navigation and safety equipment needed (see checklist on page 136). The fuel, food and water should be properly organized for the trip, and nothing should be left to chance.

If you can follow these instructions you will avoid the usual problems that most skippers and crew face from time to time – and you will probably be unique!

Coast Guard services

The United States Coast Guard (USCG) aids and protects the boating public principally in the areas of enforcement of boating regulations and safety. It makes patrols to check for reckless boat handling and hazards to navigation; it operates many aids to navigation (from unlighted buoys and daybeacons to lighthouses) as well as radiobeacons and many of the stations of the worldwide Loran-A and Loran-C system; it aids boatmen in any kind of trouble and conducts rescue operations at sea. In many of its safety functions it is assisted by its civilian support organization, the Coast Guard Auxiliary (USCG Aux), which also offers courses for the boating public and promotes education and efficiency in boat operations. The US Power Squadrons (a non-governmental private organization) also promote boating safety through education in navigation, seamanship and boat handling.

Provisioning

Provisioning the boat requires an organized mind, and one person in charge of both buying and storing the goods. Usually the skipper does it, but he can appoint someone else. You will need to see that everything for the trip – from food to the first aid kit – is on board, and it is a responsible job. If you are going to be cruising away from shore for several days, you will need a carefully worked-out menu plan so that fresh food doesn't go bad. Buy more than you need to allow for any passage-plan changes. Fresh perishable food should be stored in the coldest lockers. If possible, prepare a couple of meals at home that only need re-heating, to give yourself less to do at sea on the first day or days. Try to plan menus that are nourishing and energy-giving, and which can be prepared easily on whatever type of stove is available. Always aim to start the day with a decent breakfast, and make sure you have ingredients on board for hot snacks, for the times when weather may make it difficult to cook proper meals. Keep some high-energy food in plastic containers – biscuits and chocolate, for example.

The crew on this boat are not going to go short of food, but the bottles should be stowed in their own locker, and well-chocked to prevent breakage.

Watch-keeping

Passage making is tiring both physically and mentally and more so in rough weather. If every member of the crew is to be alert, it will be necessary for them to have sufficient sleep and rest, the skipper included. When night-sailing or in heavy weather, it is necessary to divide the crew into two groups (known as watches) and establish a watch-keeping system. This allows the boat to be adequately manned by the "duty watch" while the off-duty watch recharges its energies, asleep or resting. A crew member on duty watch who has not had sufficient sleep is a risk. It is, therefore, important to create an atmosphere below which is conducive to sleep, keeping light and noise to a minimum. The traditional 24-hour watch-keeping system is one of four hours on duty and four hours off duty, with two short dog watches when everyone is normally awake (right). Another established system, some-times known as the Swedish system, is one where the length of the watches changes between day and night (far right). For some people, the longer watch periods can prove too long. Some experienced skippers develop their own system based on one or the other and operate it successfully. It is import-ant, of course, to space meal times sensibly and to use the time when all hands are awake to carry out sail changes, for example. Seamanship experience has to be distributed between the watches and the changeover must be carried out punctually.

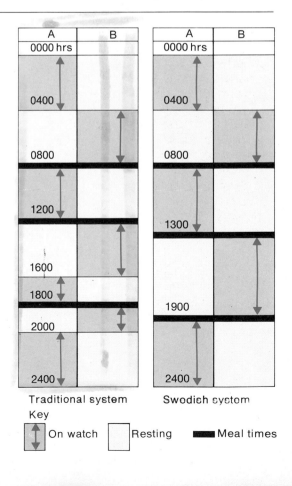

Traditional system

Swedish system

Key

↕ On watch   ☐ Resting   ▬ Meal times

THE BASIC CRUISER

Although the layout of most modern medium-sized cruising boats is broadly similar, both internally and externally, there are many variations in the detail. The number of berths will be determined largely by the size of the boat, as will the number and sophistication of the various fittings. Very small boats may not have a separate head and may only have a limited galley area. The only major difference you are likely to come across is in the siting of the cockpit. On some of the bigger boats it is in the center of the boat, rather than at the aft end. This has the advantage of providing an after cabin that is separated from the rest of the living accommodation, giving greater privacy.

As far as the external arrangement is concerned, the only obvious difference on most Marconi boats is in the size of the cabin trunk, and the position and size of the cockpit. Some boats may be steered with a wheel, others with a tiller.

The layout, right, is of a medium-sized cruiser-racer and that below of a slightly larger cruising boat.

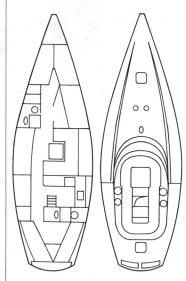

Far left, the interior layout of a fairly large cruising boat with a center cockpit. It has an aft cabin and 8 berths. The deck layout, left, apart from the siting of the cockpit in the center of the boat, is broadly similar to the cruiser-racer at right. Most larger boats, however, tend to have a wheel rather than a tiller.

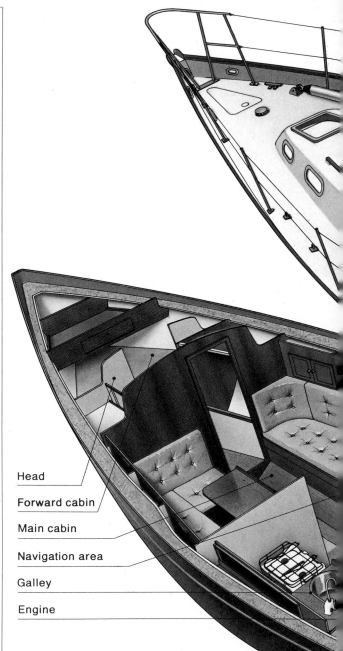

Head

Forward cabin

Main cabin

Navigation area

Galley

Engine

Interior layout

Plan of the interior of a cruiser-racer showing the accommodation split into three main areas: the forward cabin, the head and the main cabin, with the galley and navigation partly partitioned off from it.

Deck layout

Plan of a medium-sized cruiser-racer showing the deck area and cockpit layout. The number and position of the winches will vary, but they should, ideally, all be within reach of the cockpit. The boat is tiller-steered.

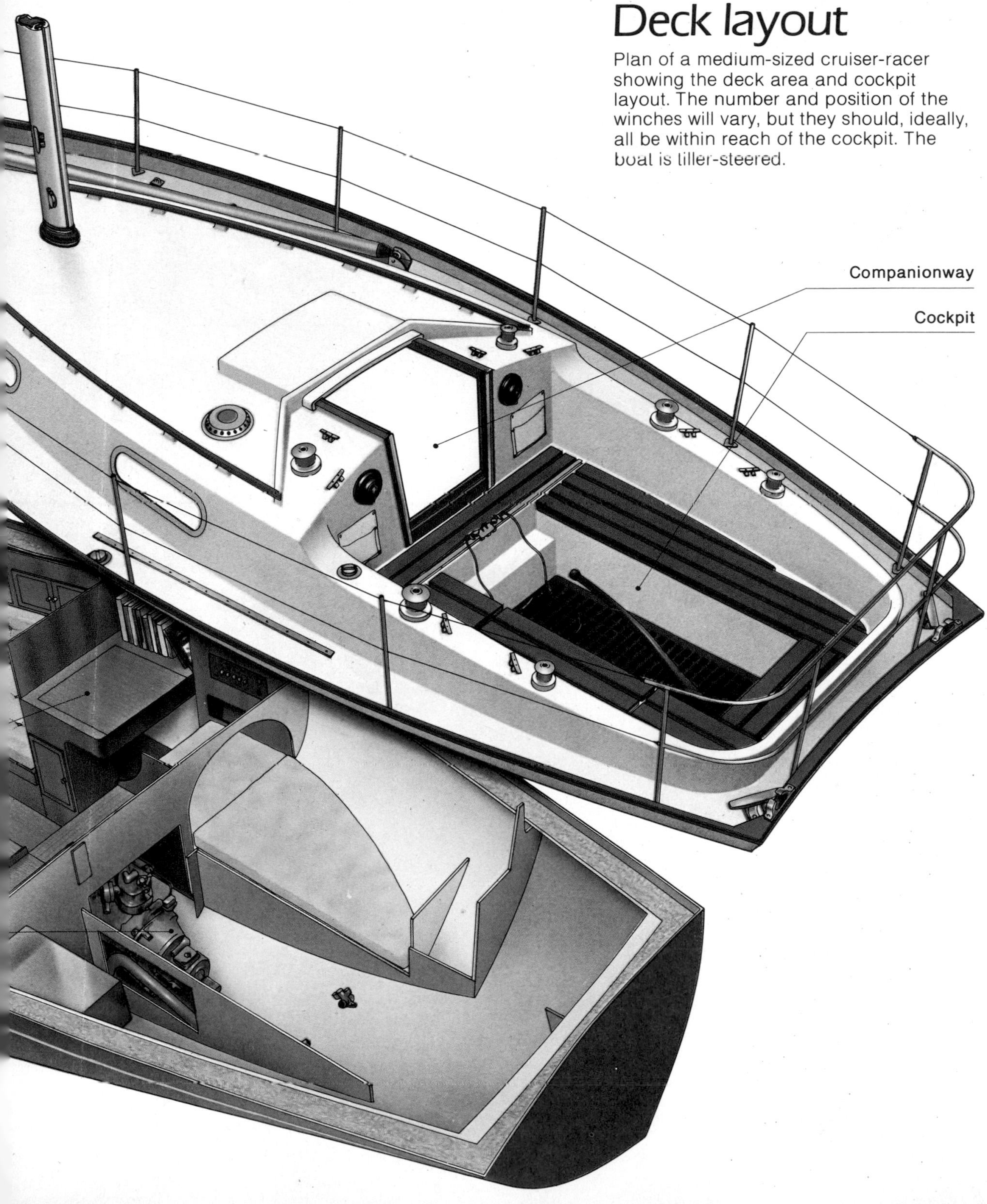

Companionway

Cockpit

TYPES OF BOAT

The cruising sailor today has an almost un-limited choice of boat, and it can be bewildering for the potential first-time buyer. No-one should rush into buying a boat. Get plenty of sailing practice in different types of boat, and find out what your particular preferences are. Think carefully about your likely needs and those of your family and crew, and the area in which you are sailing. Don't buy any boat unless you are very sure you know what you are doing, or have good professional advice.

You must consider very carefully what you are about to do when you buy a boat. What do you really want the boat for? If you expect to be sailing in a shallow water area, with your family forming your crew, and your activities limited to weekend sailing, then it would be foolish to buy a deep-keeled racing boat, simply because it looks smart and you want to impress your friends! On the other hand, if you think you may want to race quite frequently, with the occasional weekend cruise, then you should look for a proven cruiser-racer of a type which is raced in your neighborhood, so you get good competitive racing.

Cost is, of course, a crucial factor for most people, and you must bear in mind the likely running costs, as well as the initial purchase price. Small, lightweight boats will cost less initially, and will be cheaper to run than their larger counterparts. Moorings could be difficult to obtain, and possibly expensive. Trailer-sailers may overcome this problem, since they can be kept at home and towed behind the family car to different sailing areas.

Although modern boat design tends to cram a large number of berths into a small boat, some of the berths will not be usable when under way so if you are likely to do much serious cruising, plan to sail with about half the

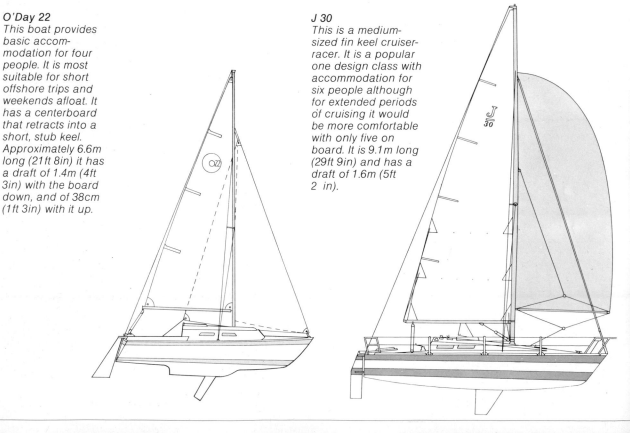

O'Day 22
This boat provides basic accommodation for four people. It is most suitable for short offshore trips and weekends afloat. It has a centerboard that retracts into a short, stub keel. Approximately 6.6m long (21ft 8in) it has a draft of 1.4m (4ft 3in) with the board down, and of 38cm (1ft 3in) with it up.

J 30
This is a medium-sized fin keel cruiser-racer. It is a popular one design class with accommodation for six people although for extended periods of cruising it would be more comfortable with only five on board. It is 9.1m long (29ft 9in) and has a draft of 1.6m (5ft 2 in).

number of people the boat is supposed, in theory, to accommodate.

The rig you choose will also depend on your requirements. These days most production boats tend to be Marconi sloop-rigged, although other rigs are gaining popularity. For someone who genuinely wants to potter about, a gaff-rigged boat may be more fun to sail than a Marconi-rigged boat (see also page 49). If you have friends and acquaintances who are experienced sailors ask their advice. Plan to spend some time at any large boat show, and visit as many stands as you can. Beg a passage on different boats and find out how they handle. Above all, don't rush into buying anything. If you find you are still in doubt, buy something you can sell again easily if you discover you don't like it!

Westerly 33
A wide-beamed 10m (33ft) family cruiser which has spacious accommodation for up to seven people. It comes in a sloop or ketch rig (as illustrated) and can be fin- or bilge-keeled. It isn't difficult to sail, and is therefore suitable for an inexperienced family crew, but is not particularly speedy. Other similar boats are the Bristol 33 and the Dufour 35.

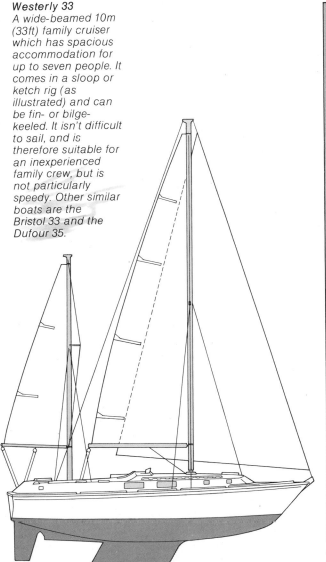

A Contessa 32, one of the most successful and popular medium-sized cruising boats.

ACCOMMODATION

In most small cruising boats you will find only the most basic fittings and comforts provided as standard by the boat builders. Anything more luxurious will be charged as an extra. Larger boats, however, tend to have a little more in the way of built-in comfort.

The organization of the accommodation will depend largely on how the boat is intended to be used. Some people plan to spend only a limited time sailing, stopping for the night in a marina or at a mooring. Although a medium-sized cruiser may well have six berths, it does not necessarily mean that you could indulge in any protracted cruising with six people on board. The forepeak berths, for example, are unpleasant to use under way because of the motion, and they are often the only place where sails can be stowed when not in use, preventing their use for sleeping accommodation. Boats that have been designed primarily for short trips often lack basic fittings which are needed at sea — leecloths on the bunks, fiddles on the flat surfaces, grabrails around the cabin, strong catches on the side lockers, an organized galley and a well-designed navigation area.

Much, therefore, depends on how you wish to use your boat. If you intend to do some serious sailing, make sure that the boat design below decks will answer your purpose.

There is often a lack of privacy on small cruisers and you may find that an arrangement with a center cockpit and aft cabin (see page 30) suits your needs better than the more common aft cockpit layout, shown below.

Interior layout

A typical below-decks layout for a medium-sized cruiser, right and below. It has six berths, two in the forward cabin, three in the main cabin and a quarter berth, partly under the cockpit. It would be comfortable for four people but might be cramped with six on board.

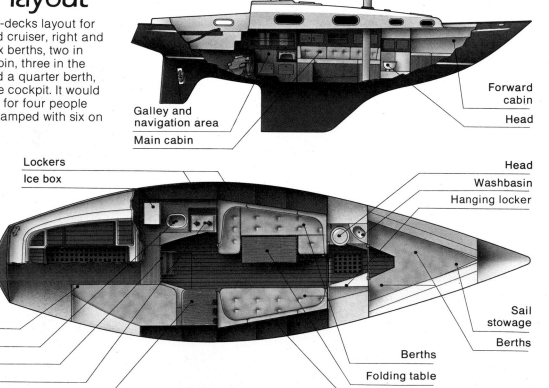

Galley and navigation area

Main cabin

Forward cabin

Head

Lockers

Ice box

Head

Washbasin

Hanging locker

Quarter berth

Sink

Companionway

Stove

Chart table

Sail stowage

Berths

Berths

Folding table

Lockers

Navigation area

The ideal place in the boat for the navigation area is close to the companionway, so that the navigator and helmsman can communicate easily. It must have a table, preferably facing forward. It should be large enough to hold an open chart, or at least one folded in half. The navigation area should also have shelving for tide tables, books and so on. The navigation equipment used by the navigator and skipper should be mounted where it can be seen easily by both of them.

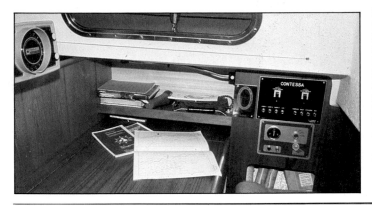

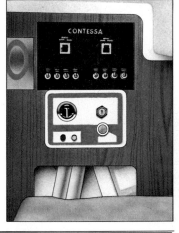

Left, the navigation area of a typical medium-sized boat. Right, the instrument panel with switches for electricity and the engine. In this layout, the batteries are under the quarter berth.

Galley

The galley should be equipped with a small stove, preferably with an oven, and fuelled if possible by bottled gas. It should either be gimballed (and able to swing freely to an angle of 60° either side of the vertical) or it should be fixed, with clamps for the pans. The galley should also have a sink with a pump-operated water supply, an ice box, and work surfaces with fiddled edges. There should also be a fire blanket and extinguisher, and a bar across the front of the stove to prevent the cook being thrown onto it.

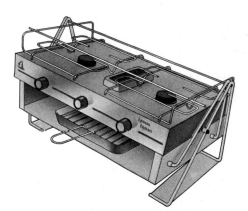

Above, a gimballed stove with pan clamps; left, galley area with stove, sink, counters and cupboards; right, ice box under the counters.

Main cabin

In almost every boat, the main cabin occupies its center and provides the main living area. In most family cruisers, it is not particularly roomy and the furniture is limited, most of the space being taken up by the berths. The cabin, right, has a double and single berth, the center cushions of the double berth masking a foldaway table (below). In traditional boats, the cabin was lined with wood whereas in most modern boats it is either wood veneer or plastic. The latter is practical but less attractive. Fittings should be flush, where possible, to minimize the likelihood of injury in rough weather.

Right, fitting a leecloth onto a berth. All berths should have a leeboard or cloth to prevent the occupant falling out when under way.

Far right, two crew members relaxing in the main cabin while a third works in the galley. Keep the cabin free of clutter; stow all equipment in the lockers.

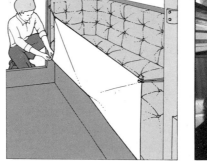

Folding table

Most small cruisers have a folding, as opposed to a fixed, table. The type below has a telescopic leg and folding top. In use, the leg is pushed up and locked in the higher position. The table unfolds to become a full-sized one. It must have fiddles around the edge.

Stowage areas

The stowage areas on board the boat are crucial to comfort when sailing. All provisions and possessions need careful organizing so that those most frequently used are in the most accessible places. In most boats there will be both high and low level stowage. All lockers should have strong catches and some of them should have interior fittings designed to hold bottles and other breakables.

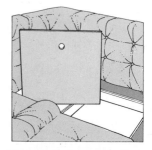

Above right, low level locker under a bunk; right, special fittings for stowing bottles and glasses.

Forward cabin

The forward cabin lies under the foredeck and usually has a double or two single berths. It is the most uncomfortable part of the boat to sleep in, as the motion is greatest at the bow. You may also find that much of the space is taken up by the sails once you are under way. However, since this will only affect your crew if you are sailing at night, when some of them will be on watch, you can usually organize things so that an off-duty member sleeps in the main cabin – known to the initiated as the "hot bunk system". The forward cabin usually has a hatch for light and ventilation. It can be used as an additional exit if a ladder is provided. Make sure the seal is watertight. There is usually a reasonable amount of stowage space below the berths which can be used for bulkier items.

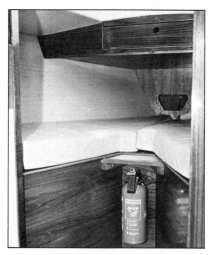 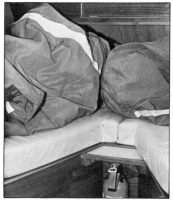

Left, two single berths in the forepeak and, above, sail bags stowed temporarily.

Care of the interior

Whether you like it or not, you are going to have to spend quite a lot of your time aboard simply looking after your boat. Keeping it clean and orderly is more than simply a matter of good looks, although pride in the appearance of your boat is important. In the damp and poorly ventilated conditions below decks, any dirt that is allowed to accumulate will soon start to form mold and begin to smell unpleasant. Before and after each trip, clean out the whole boat, leaving the lockers and stowage areas open to allow air to circulate. To keep the bilges clean, you should pump them out between trips and pour in a patent bilge cleaner occasionally. Make sure you clean up the stove and oven if you have one, and check that the gas pipe fitting, the seacocks and the heads are functioning properly. Turn off all seacocks whenever you leave the boat.

The head

Different boat designers have put the head (lavatory to landlubbers) in different positions, but the most common site is between the main and the forward cabin. The types of marine lavatory are numerous but mostly they are pump-operated. Not all harbors will allow you to use a marine lavatory discharging direct into the sea, so check the regulations first. It is vital that you know how the head works, and that you explain its operation to the crew. With some systems, an unwitting crew member could flood the boat, if seacocks (valves which control the inflow and outlet to the sea) have to be opened and closed. The head normally contains a small washbasin and a locker for oilskins.

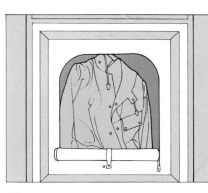

Wet clothes can be kept in the hanging locker, which drains into the bilges. A zip-fastening flap is useful.

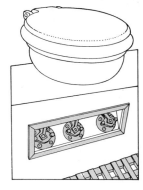

Seacocks operate the inlet and outlet pipes to the lavatory and the effluent is pumped out using a handle.

DECK EQUIPMENT

Most Marconi sloop-rigged boats have a broadly similar range of deck equipment, and the layout, below, is typical of a medium-sized cruiser. Small variations may occur in the number and siting of winches, the position of cleats and so on. If you are sailing an unfamiliar boat, get the skipper to show you around and demonstrate how the equipment works.

The fixtures and fittings have to take a considerable amount of strain so they must be robust and well-secured. Frequent mainten-ance checks are a vital safety precaution. Details of the fittings and their functions are given on the following pages.

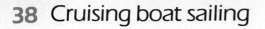

Wind indicator

Mast

Upper shroud

Headstay

Spreader

Forward lower shroud

Aft lower shroud

Navigation lights

Backstay

Main halyard winch

Topping lift

Boom

Lifeline

Headsail halyard winch

Headsail sheet winch

Spinnaker sheet winch

Cockpit

Pushpit

Navigation light

Pulpit

Anchor well

Foredeck

Forward hatch

Spinnaker pole

Cabin trunk

Grabrail

Spinnaker halyard winch

Foredeck

The foredeck of a cruiser is a potentially dangerous area. The bow of the boat suffers the greatest degree of motion in any kind of swell, and in rough seas, large waves may break over it. All the headsail changing is carried out on the foredeck, and the crew therefore needs some sort of protection while working. Normally a strong tubular steel framework, known as the pulpit, is fixed to the bow, bolted securely into the deck. The crew can brace themselves against it when working. Lifelines run from the pulpit to the stern of the boat, supported at intervals on metal stanchions. In rough weather, the crew must wear harnesses and clip themselves onto appropriate parts of the boat. Usually jacklines are rigged from eye bolts at the bow and run along each side deck to the cockpit. They are made of plastic-covered wire or of webbing, and provide a convenient clipping-on point along the length of the foredeck. The anchor is normally kept on the foredeck – in modern boats there is often a covered anchor well sunk into the foredeck, in which the anchor is stowed when not being used. There should be at least one fairlead on either side of the bow, with an accompanying cleat set slightly aft of it. The headstay, or headstays if the boat has twin ones fitted, are attached to the bow fitting.

The foredeck surface is an important factor. It should be made of non-slip material with a raised lip (or toe rail) at the outer edge to prevent the crew from slipping under the guardrails. The forward hatch can be fitted into the foredeck or in the fore part of the cabin. It must be strong, watertight, and capable of being securely locked from both inside and outside. Make sure the foredeck is free of clutter at all times. Coil up lifelines immediately after use and stow them. Bag up sails, or stow them neatly against the lifelines if they are likely to be used again shortly.

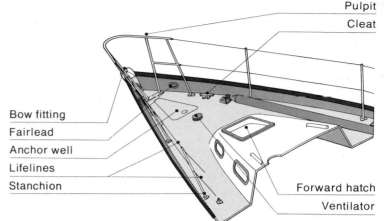

Pulpit
Cleat
Bow fitting
Fairlead
Anchor well
Lifelines
Stanchion
Forward hatch
Ventilator

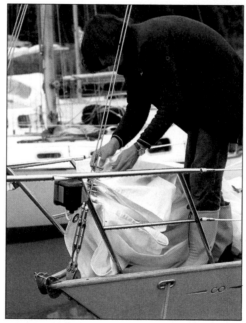

The tubular framework, known as the pulpit, surrounds the bow and provides protection for the crew when rigging or changing headsails. It must be securely through-bolted to the deck.

Lacing

To prevent the sails being blown or washed off the foredeck, most people interlace the lifelines near the bow of the boat with a thin braided cord. This not only helps protect your equipment, but provides additional security for the crew working on the foredeck.

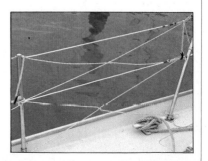

Cabin trunk

In most boats the cabin accommodation is covered over with a raised cabin trunk to give more headroom below decks. If the mast is deck stepped, the cabin trunk is normally reinforced at this point, often with a pillar support running from the deckhead to the keel. The sides of the cabin trunk normally contain small windows or port holes to allow light into the cabin below. The seal around them should be completely watertight, as should those around the ventilators, which allow air to circulate in the cabin. A forward hatch is normally incorporated into the front part of the cabin trunk to allow sails to be passed through, and to allow light and air into the forward cabin. The hatch should have a waterproof seal, and should be kept firmly closed when under way. Stanchions with lifelines are fitted around the side decks. The spinnaker pole is normally stowed along one of the side decks and the jib sheet fairleads are secured on either side deck, just forward of the cockpit. A grabrail runs around the cabin trunk.

The companionway, the access into the cabin, is usually at the aft end of the cabin trunk and can be closed by a sliding hatch and washboards (wooden partitions). The hatch should have a proper lock that can be operated from inside and out, and should be secured shut when sailing in rough conditions. The washboards should also be capable of being secured separately from inside and out. Grab handles, fitted in the companionway, and rubber treads on the steps help to provide a more secure hand- and foothold when the boat is heeling. There should be a strong fastening point near the hatchway so that harness lines can be clipped on before the crew leave the cabin.

Mast
Boom
Forward hatch
Cabin trunk
Ventilator
Grabrail
Cabin light
Spinnaker pole
Companionway
Headsail sheet lead track

Stowing on deck

Every boat should have a proper liferaft on board (see page 149) and a common place to stow it is on the cabin trunk, either forward of the mast or between the mast and the companionway. Alternatively, it could be stowed in a separate cockpit locker. If stowed on deck, it should be tied onto specially shaped chocks using a quick release knot (see page 154). If you have an inflatable tender you can stow it, deflated, alongside the liferaft. Make sure that all equipment is properly tied down, and that there are no trailing lines which might trip up an unwary crew member. Ancillary equipment, such as brooms and boat-hooks, should *not* be tied to the grabrails, as it may prevent their use as hand-holds. Stow them in a locker in the cockpit or down below.

Right, the liferaft and deflated tender stowed securely on the cabin trunk.

Mast

The majority of boats these days use aluminum masts as they are strong, light and durable. The height of the mast will depend on the size of the boat and the design of the rig. Most small cruisers have a single pair of spreaders — struts extending sideways from the mast to spread the shrouds and increase their lateral support.

The shrouds, of stainless steel or galvanized wire, are attached to chainplates mounted on the sides of the hull, or on the side decks. With a single spreader arrangement, the upper shrouds run from the masthead to the side decks and a further pair of shrouds runs from the spreader roots to the chainplates. These are called the lower shrouds. A headstay and backstay, of similar construction to the shrouds, run from the masthead to the bow and stern respectively and support the mast fore and aft. Although the shrouds have a fixed tension, the backstay can usually be adjusted when sailing. Navigation lights may be attached to the masthead, as can a wind indicator and a radio aerial. The mast usually contains the sail halyards which emerge near the deck. The appropriate winches and cleats are fixed nearby, or

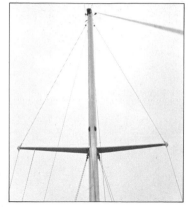

Left, the lower part of the mast seen from the side and, above, the upper part of the mast showing shrouds, spreaders and stays.

the halyards are led back to winches near the cockpit. The gooseneck fitting of the boom is mounted on the aft side of the mast. If the boat has a spinnaker, the pole bracket is mounted on the front of the mast and the spinnaker halyard winch and cleat on the side, or near the cockpit. The boom vang is usually secured to the heel of the mast on the aft side.

Boom

The boom provides rigid support for the foot of the mainsail. On modern boats it is usually made of aluminum and has a groove along the top into which the foot rope of the mainsail is inserted. The tack of the sail is secured at the gooseneck while a clew outhaul is used to adjust the tension on the foot of the sail. The boom is attached to the mast with a gooseneck fitting which may be mounted on a sliding track, so that the height of the boom can be adjusted. A boom vang fixed to the underside of the boom is used to prevent its lifting when sailing. The mainsheet is attached along the aft end of the boom; the topping lift runs from the end of the boom to the masthead and holds up the boom when the mainsail is not hoisted. If your boat has jiffy reefing equipment this will also be attached to the boom (right).

Cockpit

The cockpit is sited either at the aft end of the boat, or in the center depending on the design. It normally comprises a self-draining footwell with seating on each side. There is a rigid framework called the pushpit at the stern. Like the pulpit at the bow, it serves to protect the crew. The cockpit is the safest part of the deck for the crew, and as many of the boat controls as possible should be led back to it so that the crew can work with the maximum protection and safety. There should be a fairlead and cleat for mooring lines on each side of the cockpit at the stern. All the controls and instruments, such as compasses, depth sounders, speedometer and so on, should be easily accessible, and visible, from the helmsman's position at the tiller or wheel. The tiller can often be stowed against the backstay or pushpit when not in use giving more space in the cockpit when in harbor. The choice of tiller or wheel is a matter of personal preference, although on large boats a wheel is easier to handle.

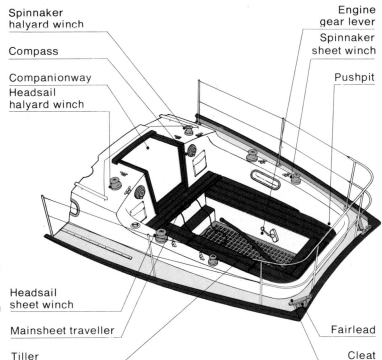

Spinnaker halyard winch

Compass

Companionway

Headsail halyard winch

Engine gear lever

Spinnaker sheet winch

Pushpit

Headsail sheet winch

Mainsheet traveller

Tiller

Fairlead

Cleat

Above, the wheel on a larger boat, with a built-in compass on a pedestal.
Left, the cockpit of a Contessa 32. It should be kept clear of lines and fenders, which should be stowed after use. Swab the decks and cockpit area regularly.

Instruments

Boat technology is rapidly improving, and the number and sophistication of the aids to navigation and steering is growing all the time. Unless you plan to do a lot of offshore cruising, you can manage quite successfully with the basic instruments (see page 128). Make sure that the compass is sited where the helmsman can see it easily when sitting on either side of the cockpit.

Stowage areas

Most boats have cockpit lockers fitted under the seating, so that large items can be stowed easily. It is best to have a separate self-draining locker for the gas cylinder. Small pockets on the sides of the cockpits are useful for stowing winch handles and other small items. Keep the equipment tidy in the lockers so that you can find what you need in a hurry.

Cockpit locker with a separate self-contained locker for the gas cylinder. Make sure the gas is turned off at the cylinder after each use, to prevent the risk of leakage.

Backstay tensioner

Most boats are fitted with an adjustable backstay which allows you to adjust the tension of both backstay and headstay, and thus the amount of sag in the jib luff. A common way of adjusting the backstay is by means of a wheel which controls a turnbuckle at the base of the stay. The backstay tension should be slackened off when the boat is not sailing.

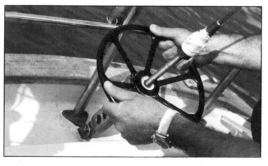

Weather protection

For the comfort of the crew in the cockpit you can fit a foldaway spray hood over the companionway, so that the hatch to it can be kept open without spray coming in below-decks. You can also fit dodgers (lengths of plastic or sailcloth) to the lifelines along the cockpit to give protection to the crew from wind and spray.

Above, dodgers on a Contessa 32 and, right, a folding spray hood

Washboards

On most boats the access to the companionway is closed by washboards. You must be able to lock them in position from the inside as well as the outside. In rough conditions, one-piece reinforced boards are better than the divided variety, below.

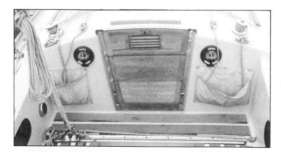

Liferings

Keep the liferings where they can be reached in an emergency. The type that have a light fitted that switches on automatically in the water are the best. You will also need a dan buoy – a floating marker used to indicate the position of a man overboard. It consists of a flag on a weighted pole with a float attached.

Left, horseshoe lifering fixed in its own bracket on the pushpit, and, right, a typical dan buoy.

WINCHES

On almost every boat over 6m (20ft) you will need winches to help you sheet in sails and tighten up halyards; they should be positioned wherever convenient to give you maximum power. There are two basic types of winch. The simpler one, the standard winch, is usually operated by two people, one of whom pulls the sheet tail around the winch drum while the other turns the winch handle. The more sophisticated variety, the self-tailing winch, has a built-in cleat, which dispenses with the need for a second person to tail on the sheet. Many winches have both a slow and fast speed; the fast speed allows the sheet to be wound in quickly when there is little strain on it and the slower speed is used when more power is needed.

Make sure you are securely positioned so that you can use the full power of your body to wind the winch.

Loading a winch

Since there is often a great deal of pressure on sheets or halyards, you may hurt your fingers badly if you do not load a winch correctly. You should always use two hands to wind the sheet on the drum, and keep the heel of your hand nearest to it so that your fingers cannot get caught between the drum and the rope. Before loading the winch, check to see which way it turns by spinning it — most winches, in fact, turn clockwise.

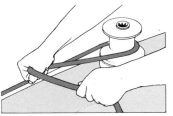

1 *Using both hands, loop the sheet around the winch in the same direction in which the drum rotates.*

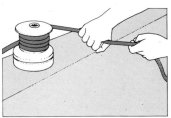

2 *Keeping the heel of your hand nearest the drum, take three or four turns around the winch before pulling on the sheet.*

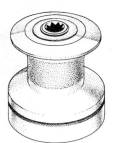

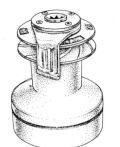

Standard winch   **Self-tailing winch**

3 *If the self-tailing winch is used, wind the tail through the self-tailing mechanism after taking three or four turns.*

4 *With three or four turns on the drum use the winch handle as necessary (opposite above). Cleat the sheet tail so it won't slip.*

Using a winch handle

Most winches are operated using a top-mounted winch handle which engages in a central socket. The ratchet mechanism then takes the strain so that you can wind in the sheet easily, even when there is considerable pressure on it. If you have a two-speed winch, the handle is usually turned clockwise for one speed, and counter-clockwise for the other.

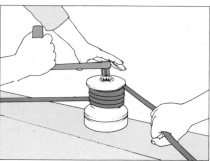

Left, make sure that you pull on the tail in a horizontal direction so as not to form riding turns.

Easing and releasing sheets

To ease the tension of a sheet on a winch, the tail of the sheet should be taken off the cleat. One hand should be kept over the turns of the winch drum to prevent them easing off too rapidly, while the other hand gradually eases the tension on the tail. To remove the sheet completely, never unwind it from the winch. Simply ease the tension first, and then tug the sheet sharply upwards by the tail, releasing it quickly when all the turns have unwound.

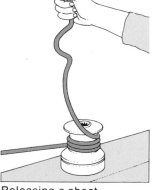

Releasing a sheet

Easing a sheet

Removing a riding turn

If you are careless when winding the sheet onto the winch, or if the angle of the sheet to the winch is wrong, you can get the coils crossed, in a riding turn. It may not be possible to undo it unless the strain is taken off the sheet. You should tie another rope to the sheet between the winch and the sheet-lead, using a rolling hitch (see page 153). The new rope is then taken around a spare winch and wound in until it is taking all the strain from the sheet. You will then find it possible to release the riding turn. Rewind the sheet and continue winching in the normal way.

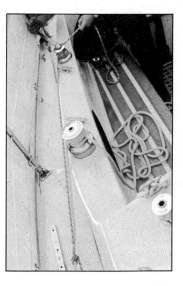

Above, a riding turn on a winch. Right, a riding turn has been produced on the winch in the foreground, and the rear winch is being used to take the strain on the new rope, in order to release the tension on the sheet.

SAILS

If you are a keen cruising sailor and want to get the best performance out of your boat, it pays to have a good set of sails, properly cut and of the appropriate design for cruising. Developments in sail-making have produced tougher and more stable cloths that hold their shape better than the earlier ones did, and modern sail design and construction have helped both to reduce distortion and to increase sail life. Although sailcloths with a hard finish are commonly used for racing, the soft-finish cloths are more suitable for cruising – the sails are easier to handle and stow, and are more durable.

Some cruising skippers mistakenly try to copy the sail wardrobes of racing boats. The requirements of cruising are quite different. Ease of handling, durability and versatility are the priorities of the cruising yachtsman, whereas the racing boat skipper can usually spend more, carry a larger sail wardrobe and concern himself solely with efficiency.

One of the questions that perennially crops up with cruising sailors is whether to carry a spinnaker. Although it is simple enough to use the engine when travelling downwind in light breezes, it is much more enjoyable, and cheaper, to use a special downwind sail, or, failing that, to pole out a genoa or boom out two headsails, one on either side of the boat. Although cruising skippers who sail regularly with a reasonably competent crew may find it worthwhile to invest in an all-round spinnaker, those with a less able crew may prefer a poleless cruising chute.

Since sails are expensive, you must look after them carefully. Don't leave them rigged and uncovered – the cloth will deteriorate if left exposed for any length of time to ultraviolet light. Be sure to cover the mainsail when you're not using the boat.

A typical cruising sail wardrobe is shown overleaf, and the essential fittings to control the sail shape are shown on pages 60–61.

Right, a cruising boat sailing on a reach during a perfect evening in the West Indies. A radial-head spinnaker is set in addition to the mainsail.

Left, a family cruising boat moving well under a light genoa and mainsail in a very gentle breeze.

Right, a specially cut reaching headsail being used to provide a cruiser with extra power in light conditions.

Sail wardrobe

The sail wardrobe your boat carries will depend on a number of factors – the rig, the relative experience of your crew, and the nature and extent of your cruising. You will have to carry a range of headsails to cover wind strengths varying from light to strong, and the number you carry will be determined by whether or not you possess a headsail reefing system. If you do, you may manage with two or three headsails. The selection shown here is a typical one for a medium-sized cruiser with a relatively experienced crew, but without headsail reefing gear. A family cruiser might dispense with the spinnaker and carry a cruising chute instead.

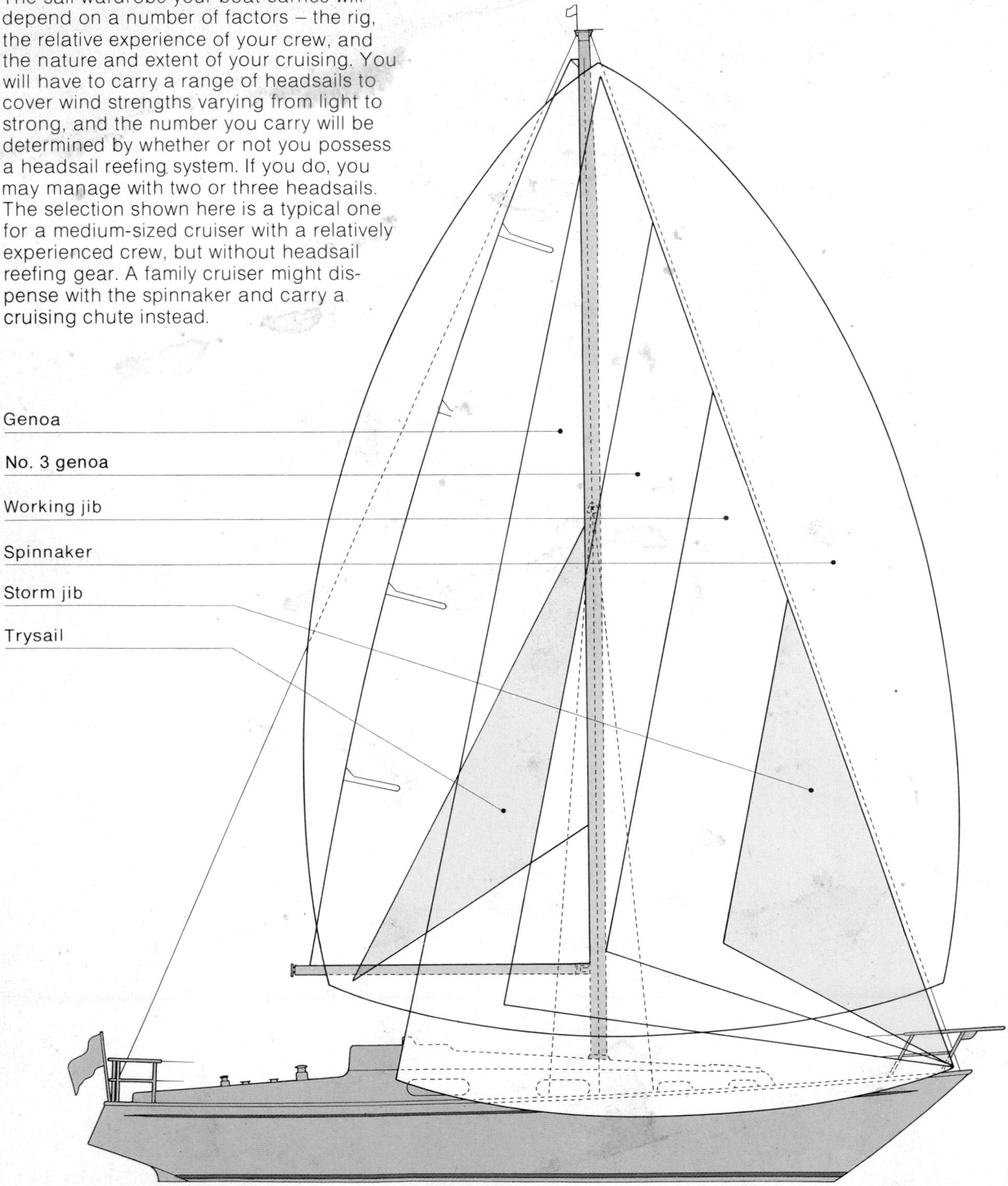

Genoa

No. 3 genoa

Working jib

Spinnaker

Storm jib

Trysail

Rig variations

Although the majority of modern cruising boats are sold with a Marconi sloop rig, there are a number of alternatives. This particular rig, although very efficient on windward courses, relies on large head-sails for power offwind. Short-handed crews sometimes find the large genoas difficult to handle unless a furling system is fitted. Other rigs, like the wishbone and the junk rig, which are unstayed, are easier to handle, although the junk is less efficient than the Marconi rig. The traditional gaff rig, which sails well offwind, is making a minor comeback. The ways in which the sail area can be divided up are numerous. Some people prefer a variation of the Marconi rig, such as the cutter, which carries two headsails, or the ketch or yawl rigs, which split the sail area between two masts. It all hangs on personal taste, and the kind of sailing you are likely to go in for, as well as the type of waters you will be sailing in. In general, though, the Marconi is the most versatile rig.

The traditional rig of this gaff cutter still has its adherents, and is now being used on modern fiberglass boats. It sails better offwind than it does to windward.

The junk rig, above, is not as efficient to windward as a Marconi-rigged sloop but it is easy to handle, and to reef, and sails well enough off the wind.

Two very different ways of splitting up the sail area: the boat on the right of the picture is a Marconi-rigged yawl, the boat left of picture is a modern unstayed wishbone ketch rig, a relatively new and easy-to-handle arrangement.

DINGHIES

All cruising boats need to have a dinghy to ferry the crew and stores between the boat and the shore. Ideally, it should be large enough to carry all the crew, the provisions and any sailing gear, while remaining easy to handle under both oars and an outboard motor. It should also have permanent buoyancy and be tough enough to withstand rough treatment. In practice, the problems of stowing a tender on board a small or medium-sized cruiser limit the choice of type. While the old-fashioned rigid dinghy handles better in the water, you can normally stow it only on davits (below right). The alternative is to tow it, which reduces your boat speed and causes problems when sailing in rough weather.

Most people, in fact, opt for an inflatable dinghy which can be partially deflated and easily stowed on deck or in a large locker. They are not easy to row in a strong wind, and you may find that you need an outboard motor for long trips. Inflatables, being soft, have the advantage that they don't damage the boat when coming alongside.

You should be very careful when using the dinghy – more drownings result from their misuse than from people going overboard from a cruiser. Make sure that crew members wear a lifejacket in the dinghy, even on short trips, and even if they can swim. Never overload the tender – make two trips, if necessary.

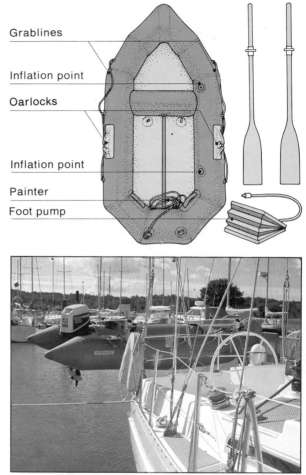

Grablines

Inflation point

Oarlocks

Inflation point

Painter

Foot pump

Towing a dinghy

If you have a rigid dinghy you probably have to tow it behind you boat, at least for short trips. Even if you have an inflatable you may prefer to tow it occasionally rather than deflate it and stow it, if you know you are going to use it again shortly. Before setting off, remove all the loose gear from the dinghy and stow it aboard the boat. Use a strong warp as a towing line, making sure that it is long enough to allow the dinghy to lie well astern of the boat. The line should be fixed to a through-bolted eye on the outside of the stem of the dinghy. A slack reserve line should be fastened from the dinghy to the boat just in case the towing line breaks. In strong winds you may find that an inflatable dinghy becomes airborne or even blows aboard the boat. Under

these conditions, shorten the towing line right up so that the inflatable's bow is out of the water, near the boat's transom. You may also need a shorter line when towing a dinghy in harbor. A rigid dinghy is, in fact, more difficult to tow than an inflatable. It sometimes tends to surf down a wave when the boat is sailing offwind, and crash into the boat. In this case, you should lengthen the line even though the dinghy may sheer about as a result.

If you are maneuvering in congested waters, a crew member should look after the dinghy to ensure that the towing line doesn't foul the propeller or rudder, and that the dinghy doesn't hit any other boats. Never try to board the dinghy when under way, for whatever reason.

Using a dinghy

Dinghies, whether inflatable or rigid, are inherently unstable, and you should take great care when using them. Be particularly careful getting in and out of the dinghy to avoid upsetting it. After launching it in the water, secure the painter to a stanchion base or deck cleat near the shrouds.

The oarsman should get in first, stepping into the middle of it, and sitting down immediately on the central thwart, facing the stern. The oars are passed to him, followed by any stores being transported. Make sure the weight is distributed evenly. Any other passengers should then get in, taking care to balance the dinghy, and holding it steady against the sides of the cruiser. When the oarsman has fitted the outboard oar into its oarlock, and has said he is ready, the crew member nearest the painter casts off and pushes the dinghy clear so that the oarsman can fit the other oarlock and oar.

To disembark, simply reverse the order of getting in, taking care to keep the weight balanced.

If you are coming ashore in tidal water, make sure your dinghy is pulled up above the high water mark if there is an incoming tide. If coming ashore in an unfamiliar estuary or river, watch out for deep mud. Use the slipway if there is one.

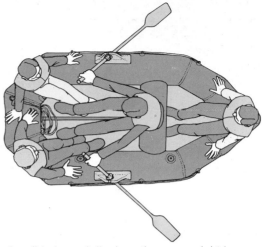

A well-balanced dinghy – the crew weight is evenly distributed. Take care to distribute stores in the same manner.

The last passenger getting into the waiting dinghy: the oarsman and crew are correctly positioned balancing the boat to receive the weight.

Rowing a dinghy

Rowing a loaded dinghy is hard work, and the oarsman must therefore be competent. If the waters are tidal, work out your plan of approach to your boat or to the shore, depending on the direction and strength of the current. Remember that it is always strongest at the point mid-way between high and low tide. It is also worth re-membering that the current is usually weaker in shallow water.

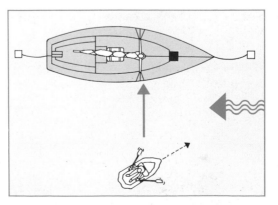

Left, if a strong current is flowing, always allow for it, to avoid being swept past your objective. Your own efforts, plus the force of the current, should push you sideways to the boat.

HANDLING LINES

The running rigging of the boat is usually made of rope (although parts of the halyards may be of wire), and since sails have to be hoisted and lowered rapidly, and mooring lines rigged quickly, you must be able to handle line correctly. The types of line and the different knots that can be used are explained on pages 150–55. However, you also need to know how to coil line so that it doesn't twist and become difficult to unravel. Any surplus line should always be coiled up neatly, never left lying in a tangle on the deck where it could trip someone up. You may also occasionally have to throw a line to the shore or to another boat (known as heaving a line). If you do not do this correctly, the line will tangle and fall short of the objective. If you are skippering a boat with an inexperienced crew on board, give them some instruction in line handling before setting sail.

Right, lines drying out on the boom. Never stow them wet – it will shorten the life of the lines, and the lockers will start to smell unpleasant!

Cleating a line

It is essential to cleat a line correctly or it may slip off or jam immovably. The cleat, of course, must be large enough to take the line, and with no sharp edges on which it could chafe. Lead the line first to the part of the cleat farthest away from it. Then take one full turn around the base of the cleat, before making a figure eight turn by winding the line over one horn of the cleat and diagonally across the cleat to make another turn on the opposite horn. You can then finish off with a final full turn around the cleat, or you can make a locking turn with a loop (below) or a half-hitch.

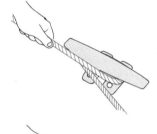

1 *Lead the line to the back of the cleat and take a turn around the base.*

2 *Make several figure eight turns around the cleat.*

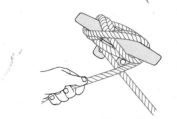

3 *Finish off with a full turn around the base of the cleat.*

Left, with synthetic mooring line, you may find it better to add a locking turn to the final figure eight. Simply slip a loop through an additional turn on the cleat, or pull the end through to form a half-hitch.

Coiling a line

Always coil any spare line neatly and secure it. There are several methods for securing a coil of line. If you are coiling and stowing a spare line, make the coils as shown in step 1, right, leaving about 2m (6ft) of the end free. Wrap the end of the rope several times around the middle of the coil, loop the end and pass it through the coil, and drop it back over the top. If you are securing the line on a cleat, use the method shown below.

1 *Hold the line in one hand close to the cleat and coil the surplus in a clockwise direction, making a clockwise twist as you form each loop, so that the coil lies flat.*

2 *Continue forming loops until all the line is neatly coiled.*

3 *Pass your hand through the coil and grasp the part leading from the cleat.*

4 *Pull this part back through the coil and twist it two or three times.*

5 *Hang the loop on the top horn of the cleat The coil will then hang neatly down from it.*

Heaving a line

You may often need to heave a line to someone on another boat or on shore. Always coil the line anew – don't rely on a previously coiled line which may be twisted or kinked. You should also check first that the line is long enough to reach the objective before throwing it. Coil the line clockwise in the usual way, making a clockwise twist in each loop so

that the coils lie flat. If you are right-handed, stand with your left shoulder towards your objective, divide the coil evenly into two parts and hold one in each hand. Then throw the coil in your right hand, swinging your arm back in an underarm motion, and aiming slightly higher than the objective. Release the remaining coils, but hold onto the end!

1 *Divide the correctly formed coils into two parts, holding one in each hand.*

2 *Swing your throwing arm back in an underarm arc, and aim slightly higher than your objective.*

3 *Release the coil in your throwing hand, and let the remainder of the coil in your other hand run free.*

BOAT HANDLING UNDER POWER

Almost every modern cruising boat is fitted with an engine – usually an inboard on larger boats and an outboard on smaller boats. The engine is normally used only for maneuvering in harbors, or for making a port if the wind drops. The engine is also a useful safety precaution – it can be used to get a cruising boat out of trouble, when fighting a foul tide or trying to reach a port before a storm. Cruising skippers should beware of relying on their engines, and should certainly feel confident that they can handle the boat under sail in any of the situations in which they might use the engine, in case of unexpected engine failure. If you are using the engine make sure that the sails are ready for immediate hoisting and the anchor is also made ready in case of just such an emergency.

In close quarters, the skipper must retain complete control of his boat at slow speeds.

Types of engine

You have a choice of inboard or outboard engine for your boat. Normally larger boats have an inboard, and smaller one an outboard. The former is often mounted under the cockpit floor, and the latter on the transom of the boat. Both types need proper attention, regular servicing and maintenance. As with all machinery, you should take care when using it. The outboard engine is more vulnerable to the elements than the inboard (and to possible damage) but these days solid-state ignitions and improved combustion, coupled with better resistance to corrosion, have improved the reliability of both types of engine. Your engine should have a handbook which gives detailed illustrations of the parts and the main servicing points. Keep the handbook on board in an accessible place and make sure that any servicing instructions are carried out. Keep an adequate stock of spares on board. Engines are either two-stroke, using a gas-oil mixture or four-stroke, using gas or diesel fuel. Take care to use the right fuel for the engine and, in the case of the two-stroke, the right ratio of gas to oil. Apart from regular servicing and maintenance while the engine is in use in the sailing season, you will have to take care of it in the winter months when not using the boat. The engine should be overhauled, drained and cleaned and laid up in a warm dry place with a protective cover. When you recommission the engine, take care to follow the instructions.

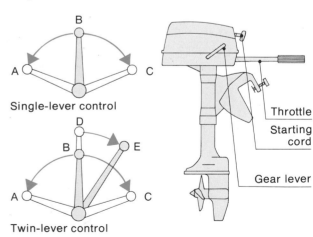

Single-lever control

Twin-lever control

Inboard engines usually have single-lever or twin-lever gear controls. The single throttle and gear control combined is operated by pushing the lever from neutral (B) towards C for forward gear (the farther you push, the more acceleration) and towards A for reverse.

With the twin-lever type, the throttle is a separate lever (D to E). An outboard works by using a similar two-gear control and a separate throttle which twists to increase or reduce speed. The inboard is normally started with an ignition key, the outboard with a cord attachment.

Propeller effects

The action of the blades of the propeller in the water produces both forward movement and a certain amount of lateral movement as well. This lateral movement is usually described as prop walk. It follows the direction in which the propeller rotates, so a boat with a clockwise-rotating propeller will find its stern moving to starboard a little as it goes forward. Since the propeller blades turn in the opposite direction in reverse, you will find that the stern moves to port in reverse gear. You will find that the effect of prop walk is most pronounced at slow speeds, and in reverse. It is vital to know which direction the prop walk on your engine takes, so that you can make allowances for it when maneuvering your boat.

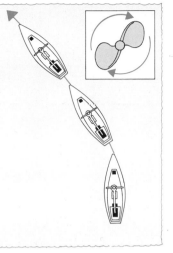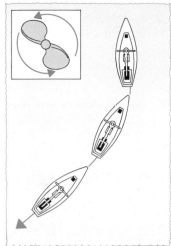

If the boat has an engine with a clockwise-rotating propeller, in forward gear the stern of the boat will swing to starboard and the bow to port.

In reverse, it rotates counter-clockwise, and the stern swings to port and the bow to starboard.

Using an engine

You can use the prop walk on your boat to your advantage since the boat turns a tighter circle in the opposite direction to that in which the propeller rotates – if you have a clockwise-rotating propeller your boat will turn a tighter circle to port than to starboard. The effect is even more pronounced in reverse gear, to the point where the opposite applies; you may actually find it difficult to make a turn in the same direction as the propeller rotates, unless you have quite a lot of way on. If this is the case, your only solution is to maneuver the boat using alternate short hard bursts on the throttle in forward gear with ones in reverse gear, keeping the tiller or wheel hard over in the same direction throughout the maneuver. Don't forget that at slow speeds your boat will have a tendency to drift as well, and you have to take this into account in your planning. If the propeller shaft is not positioned centrally, but more to one side of the boat or the other, then you will find that there is a pronounced tendency for the bow of the boat to turn away from the side on which the propeller is mounted when in forward gear, and for the boat to do the opposite in reverse. If your boat has this problem, then make sure the propeller

rotates in the opposite direction so that it counterbalances the off-center effect rather than exacerbates it. Remember that when a boat backs up, its rudder works the opposite way – to swing the stern to port, the tiller goes to starboard. In other words, the stern goes the way the rudder is pointed. At very slow speed, though, the rudder may have less effect than prop walk and windage.

A boat with a clockwise-rotating propeller turns using prop walk and downwind drift. Having reversed directly upwind (2–4), the boat goes ahead with the tiller hard over the other way (4–6) to complete the turn.

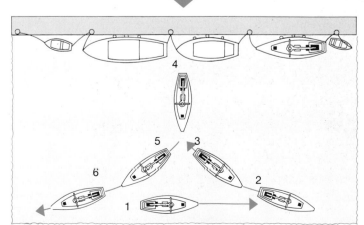

HANDLING HEADSAILS

Most cruising boats carry several headsails which are suitable for different conditions. They are all rigged in much the same way, although the individual design of the headstay system to which they are attached may vary from boat to boat. Some boats have a hank system and others a foil and groove one. Foil systems usually enable a second sail to be hoisted before the other is lowered.

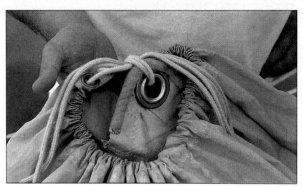

Bagged-up headsail with the tack protruding from the bag, so that it can be rigged without difficulty.

Rigging

1 The tack of the headsail is pulled out of the bag and attached to the bow fitting, usually with a snap shackle or hook fitting.

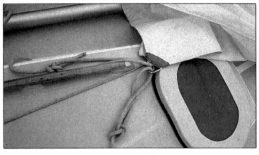

2 The crew then attaches the hanks to the forestay working up the luff taking care not to twist it as each hank is fastened.

3 The sheets are then attached to the clew of the sail with bowlines and led back along the side-decks, through the fairleads, to the cockpit. The ends are finished with figure eight knots.

Hoisting

The headsail can be hoisted on any point of sailing. When fastening the head of the sail to the halyard, take care that the halyard is not twisted around the headstay. Make sure you do not overhoist the sail – it should be tight enough to remove any horizontal creases on the luff but not so tight that a vertical crease forms when the sail is sheeted in.

1 Fasten the sail head to the halyard, having first checked that the halyard is not twisted around the headstay.

2 Uncleat the headsail halyard, take a turn around the winch and hoist the sail by hand, using the winch handle for the last few feet only. Once the sail is hoisted, cleat and coil the remaining halyard.

Lowering

It is normally easier to lower a headsail with two crew members working together as a team. One crew member is stationed at the bow while the other releases the halyard. The bow crew member gathers in the folds of the headsail as it descends, to prevent it dropping into the water. The halyard should be removed once the headsail is down, and stowed in its usual place. The sail can then be stowed temporarily or bagged up, as appropriate.

Left, a crew member gathering in the folds of the headsail. He is wearing a harness and has clipped himself on to allow both hands to be used for the job.

Using headfoils

Some modern boats are fitted with twin grooved headfoils instead of a single headstay on which the sail is hanked. The luff of the headsail is inserted into the groove in the headfoil after being put into a feeder, and it can then be hoisted quickly and easily. The main advantage of a twin headfoil system is that it gives you better boat control and speed during headsail changing, as you can hoist a second sail before lowering the first.

Stowing

When not in use, a headsail must be stowed neatly. For temporary stowage, it can be folded along the lifelines, and tied down with shock cord, to prevent it from blowing away. Alternatively, it can be stowed in its bag while still attached to the headstay. The bag is tied on to the headstay. For permanent stowage, the sail must be properly bagged up, with the tack of the sail protruding through the top, and the cord of the bag fastened through the tack eye to secure it. Try not to stow sails wet, and whenever possible let them dry out first before bagging them up. Make sure that the bag of each headsail is clearly marked with the headsail name and number on the outside.

Below, another form of temporary stowage – the headsail is being folded and tied down along the lifelines using shock cord.

Above, headsail temporarily bagged up while attached to the headstay.

Headsails for groove systems are flaked into a long sausage-shaped bag, from which the sail can be hoisted directly.

54820

HANDLING THE MAINSAIL

The mainsail of a cruiser is normally left rigged on the boom for short periods. When you do have to rig the mainsail, however, you will find it easier with two people. Don't forget to insert the battens. The method you use to stow, or furl, the mainsail depends on whether it is attached to the mast with slides or runs up it in a groove. If the former, the sail can be furled as shown opposite. If the sail has no slides on the mast it will have to be flaked back and forth in shallow folds across the boom and tied up with sail ties, called stops. On some small cruisers with roller reefing, the sail is simply rolled around the boom.

Left, a covered mainsail fastened with ties. Although the mainsail can be left uncovered and secured with shock cord for short periods, it must be covered if being left for any length of time.

Rigging

The clew end of the foot is fed into the track on the boom, and pulled along until all the foot is in the track. The tack is then fastened at the gooseneck and the clew outhaul tensioned and secured. The mainsail luff, or slide fittings if it has them, are fed into the mast track. There should be a mast gate fitted to the mast track to prevent the slides dropping out of the base of the track.

Above, the foot of the sail being pulled along the track in the boom.

Left, the clew outhaul fastened to the boom end and to the clew of the sail.

Right, the slides on the luff of the mainsail being fitted into the mast track. Don't forget to close the mast gate when they are all inserted.

Hoisting

The wind must be forward of the beam before the sail is hoisted, or it will fill with wind. Shackle the main halyard to the head, checking first to make sure that it is not fouled aloft, and then release the sail ties or shock cord around the mainsail. If the sail fits into a groove on the mast, a crew member may be needed to feed it in. Haul on the mainsail halyard, taking a turn around the winch, until the sail is pulled most of the way up the mast. Use the winch handle to fully hoist the sail, taking care not to overtension it. Ease off the topping lift and stow the surplus halyard neatly.

Fastening the head of the mainsail to the halyard.

Hoisting the mainsail up the last part of the mast using the winch handle.

Lowering and stowing

To lower the mainsail, the wind must be forward of the beam, and the mainsheet should be eased to allow the sail to flap. Don't forget to tighten the topping lift before releasing the halyard, or the boom will come crashing down on the cabin trunk. As one member eases the halyard, the other gathers in the mainsail and stows it. How you stow the mainsail depends to some extent on the type of system the boat carries. If the sail is attached to the mast with slides you will normally use the folding method, shown below, taking care not to bend the battens as you do so. Tie the sail down with shock cord or sail ties when it is neatly furled.

Left, a crew member lowering the mainsail after having lightened the topping lift.

Far left, a portion of the sail leech has been used to form a pocket into which the folds of the sail can be stowed.

Left, folded into a neat sausage-shaped bundle, the sail can be secured with sail ties or shock cord around the boom.

SAIL CONTROLS

Every cruising boat is equipped with various form of sail control. The sophistication of the equipment will depend on how much you want to spend. For most cruising boats nothing very elaborate is usually either needed or wanted. However, it is a help if the mainsheet is mounted on an adjustable traveller so that you can control the amount of downward tension on the sail, and the angle of the sail to the centreline of the boat. A boom vang is also needed to exert downward pressure on the boom and mainsail, and a downhaul and outhaul can be fitted to the luff and leech of the sail respectively to tension the luff and the foot of the mainsail. Battens can be used to stiffen the leech of the sail and adjustable fairleads can be fitted through which the headsail sheets can be led to give a better set to the sail.

Boom vang

Most cruising boats need a boom vang with a purchase power of at least six to one, preferably with the end of the purchase led to a winch to give greater power. If no boom vang is fitted, power will be lost when sailing offwind as the leech of the sail will twist forward, and the boat will roll when broad reaching or running. A tightened boom vang will effectively stop this, by preventing the boom from rising and falling, which causes the sail to chafe on the shrouds and spreaders. Increased purchase on the boom vang allows the mainsheet to be used mainly for lateral control.

A long tail on the purchase of the boom vang, above, allows a winch to be used to increase the power when needed.

Mainsheet system

The mainsheet controls the angle of the mainsail to the centerline of the boat, and is often mounted on a traveller running on an athwartships track. The traveller gives greater control over the sheeting angle and over the leech tension. In light winds it should be set to windward of the centerline and the mainsheet eased to put the boom in the center of the boat and thus produce an even curve on the leech of the mainsail. In moderate winds, the traveller should be set in the center and the mainsheet tension adjusted to keep the top batten parallel with the boom. In stronger winds, the traveller should be eased to leeward with the mainsheet kept tight, to reduce the amount of heeling force on the boat. You will find it easier to gauge the leech tension if tell-tales are used. It will be correct when all tell-tales stream aft.

Mainsheet travellers, like the one right, are now a standard fitting on many cruisers.

Luff tension

The luff of the mainsail should always be just tight enough for any horizontal wrinkles to be removed, but not so tight that a vertical crease forms near the mast. The luff tension affects the way the sail performs: when it is eased, the point of maximum draft moves aft and when it is tightened it moves farther forward. Ideally the point of maximum draft should be where the sailmaker intended it to be in moderate winds. In stronger winds you should increase the luff tension and in lighter airs you should reduce it. You can use the mainsail halyard, a Cunningham hole and tackle near the tack, or a boom downhaul and sliding gooseneck to tension the luff of the sail.

Clew outhaul

The clew outhaul affects the amount and position of the camber in the sail. By tightening the outhaul you can pull the point of maximum draft farther aft, and thus flatten the sail or you can ease the outhaul and move it forward, thus giving more fullness to the sail. Ideally, the outhaul should be tensioned just enough to prevent vertical creases appearing in the sail, but not so much that a horizontal crease is formed. The outhaul should be eased in light winds and tensioned in stronger winds.

Battens

Battens are used to support the curved leech of the mainsail and can greatly affect its shape. Those not designed to be full-length should be tapered at the inner end so that when the sail is set no hard spot is formed at the inner end of the batten pocket. If such a spot occurs, the batten is too thick and should be exchanged for a more tapered one. Full-length battens normally have some means by which the tension on them can be increased or reduced.

Leech line

On many cruising boats a thin line, known as a leech line, is threaded down the leech of the mainsail or the jib. It can be used to control any flutter or flap in the edge of the leech by increasing the tension upon it. However, care should be taken not to overtension it to the point where the leech area distorts and curves to windward. Since you sometimes get leech flutter only in a reefed mainsail, in the upper part of the sail, you can fit a leech line with an adjustment point above each reef point, so that it can be tensioned as necessary to remove the flutter.

Right, leech line in a headsail being adjusted (the crew should have clipped on a lifeline).

Headsail sheet fairleads

The position of the headsail sheet fairlead is crucial to the good set and performance of the headsail, and therefore it is important to have an adjustable headsail sheet fairlead sited on a track, so that the sheeting position can be altered for the different sizes of headsail. The fairlead should be positioned so that when the sail (regardless of size), is sheeted in for a close-hauled course, it has the same curve across it at the foot as it does at the head. The leech of the sail should have an even curve, matching the curve on the leeward side of the mainsail. On most boats the leech of an overlapping headsail, when fully sheeted, should be within 15cm (6in) from the end of the spreader. If the fairlead is set too far aft, the foot of the sail will be over-tensioned while the leech will drop off to leeward, reducing the driving power in the top of the sail. On the other hand if the lead is too far forward, too much tension will be put on the leech, causing it to hook in, but not enough will be put on the foot. The sail will be too full and the boat will heel more.

Headsail luff tension

Much the same rules apply to the headsail luff tension as to the mainsail. Normally on a cruising boat the halyard is the only control for adjusting headsail luff tension, although some boats which race have a Cunningham hole and tackle fitted to give finer adjustment. Generally you will have to use the headsail halyard, taking care not to overtension it in light airs, and to tension it enough in heavy weather.

Tell-tales

Every headsail in your sail wardrobe should be fitted with tell-tales – lengths of wool or ribbon about 30cm (12in) long, stitched through the sail and knotted on either side, so that 15cm (6in) lies on each side of the sail. Normally they should be positioned about 15cm (6in) aft from the luff of the sail, with three or four of them down the length of the luff. By attaching tell-tales you will be able to check that your sheeting angle is correct and you will also have a useful steering aid. To check the sheeting angle, sail the boat on a close-hauled course and see if all the tell-tales stream aft. If they do the angle is correct. If the top tell-tales flutter while those lower down stream correctly, the lead is too far aft, and if the reverse occurs the lead is too far forward. Provided you have the sheeting angle correct you can also use the tell-tales as a steering aid. If you are sailing to windward with the sheet properly trimmed the tell-tales on both sides of the sail should stream aft evenly. Although those on the windward side of the sail can lift slightly, they should not flutter: that means the sail is trimmed in too far or that you are sailing too close to the wind so that the sail is stalling. If the leeward tell-tales flutter, you must let out the sail or bear away until they stream aft evenly. Provided you watch the tell-tales carefully you should get the boat to point well to windward.

POINTS OF SAILING

The aim of most cruising sailors is to travel safely and enjoyably from port to port. To the cruising family, Force 5 (19 knots) can be reckoned to be a yachtsman's gale, since travelling starts to get uncomfortable at that point. Waves of about 2m (6ft) or more begin to form, spray gets thrown aboard and the crew begins to grow cold and uncomfortable.

Any cruising skipper worth his salt tries to plan his journey not only to get from one port to another with maximum speed and efficiency, but with some regard for the comfort of his crew. The downwind courses are by far the least tiring when the breeze starts to freshen up. At a gentle Force 2 (5 knots), the boat will sail upright on almost all courses, but at Force 5 (19 knots) the boat will heel on windward and reaching courses, and sail-changing becomes difficult as the bow dips and rises on increasingly large waves.

The skipper must take all these factors into account when planning a cruise, and must bear in mind the likely limitations of his crew when sailing in stiffer weather.

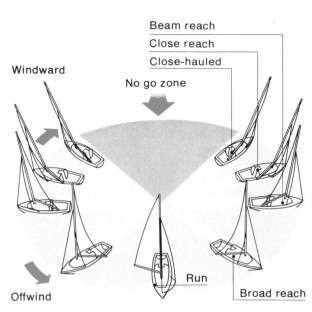

The boat can sail on any course relative to the wind, except at an angle closer than about 40° to the true wind, on either tack. How close your boat can sail depends mostly on the type of rig and design, and partly on your own skill as a helmsman. Some boats are built for efficient sailing to windward, others are built for maximum efficiency offwind, the most comfortable point of sailing for a cruising boat.

Beam reach

On this course your boat sails at right angles to the wind, which, of course, blows directly over the side of the boat. The mainsail should be set at an angle of about 45° to the centerline of the boat, well clear of the cockpit, and angled over the side of the boat. If the boat has a mainsheet traveller, move it to the leeward end of its travel. The fittings which you have for adjusting the sail shape — clew outhaul, tack downhaul or Cunningham eye — should be eased off to make the sail slightly fuller and baggier. Your headsail should operate most efficiently on a beam reach, with a nicely curved leech. Some headsails set better by moving the sheet forward to tighten the leech a little. Your aim is to get the sail to set as far away from the mainsail as possible, so that air flows quickly and smoothly over the aft end of the mainsail. The angle of the sail to the wind should be approximately the same all the way up the sail.

Close reach

The close reach is halway between close-hauled and a beam reach, and is an excellent point of sailing for even the slowest cruising boats or motor sailers. The reason for this is that the sails can be set to produce considerable forward drive without inducing much leeway. Also the majority of cruising boats, which are in the 8 to 12m (25 to 40ft) range, tend to fit neatly into the wave pattern generated in coastal waters by winds up to Force 6 (25 knots) because they are travelling diagonally across them. Progress is not impaired by having to battle through head seas, as it is when sailing closer to the wind. Because the boat is moving towards the wind, the apparent wind speed increases and its direction is modified. Sails have to be hardened in closer to the centerline of the boat, until they set correctly. In all but the lightest of breezes, they must be flattened off by increasing the tension of the sail controls. The boom will naturally lie over one end of the athwartships track, enabling effective control over the leech shape to be exercised with mainsheet tension. Your headsails should be set with the sheet fairlead in the close-hauled position (see page 61).

Close-hauled

The majority of cruising skippers dislike this point of sailing, with reason. By definition a cruising boat is a mobile home, and by design it is a load carrier with a moderate sail area. Even most racing cruisers have additional weight in the form of proper accommodation, water, fuel and stores. Close-hauled courses indicate that the boat is sailing as close to the wind as shape, ballast, sail area, leeway and human skill will allow. This will vary from 35° for a cruiser-racer to 45 to 50° for a motor sailer. You often hear close-hauled sailing described as "beating" or "punching to windward", revealing the true characteristics of the course in wind conditions stronger than Force 4 (14 knots). Apart from the fact that great concentration is required on the part of the helmsman, boat speed is lost as the hull forces its way through the wave crests moving towards it. Many of the waves splash aboard even in moderate winds, and will probably break over the bows in stronger winds. The boat will heel at 20 to 25° or more, making crew movement difficult above and below decks.

In all but the lightest of airs the sail controls should be set to flatten the sails. The mainsheet traveller should be set in the center of the track, and the boom vang should be fully tensioned. In very light winds, the traveller should be taken to the windward end of the track and the mainsheet eased to center the boom. Obviously there are occasions when the skipper has no choice but to sail close-hauled in unpleasant

The Contessa 32, left, is sailing well to windward in light airs, with the sails set to produce maximum drive.

conditions, but in the main it is to be avoided. If you have to change sails, or take in a reef when sailing close-hauled, you might consider heaving-to, if you have an inexperienced crew aboard. They should be asked to wear safety harnesses, properly clipped on, in wind strengths over Force 4 (14 knots).

Broad reach

The broad reach is one of the most enjoyable points of sailing, with the boat moving at its maximum speed for the given conditions. To judge for yourself, try sailing close-hauled in a Force 5 (19 knots) and then bear away on a broad reach. The contrast is so marked that it is difficult to believe you are out on the same day. The difference can also be seen if two boats meet, one beating to windward, the other broad reaching. The crew of the reaching boat will be relaxing in the cockpit whereas the close-hauled boat crew will be encased in waterproofs, sheltering under the cockpit hood to avoid the spray.

To get the best out of broad-reaching courses, the boom needs to be held down by a tightly tensioned boom vang, but the other sail shape controls should be eased to give the sail plenty of shape. The mainsheet traveller should be at the leeward end of the track, and the headsail sheet lead taken forward. In boisterous seas, you might find it better to rig a boom preventer of some description (see page 71) to steady the boom when the boat rolls.

Running

You may think this is the most direct and fastest course to your objective, but this is not always the case. The apparent wind is the least you will encounter because the boat is moving away from the wind, and the mainsail tends to blanket the headsail. You will also find the boat difficult to steer because any fluctuations in wind direction could result in an accidental jibe. When sailing directly downwind, you will need to have a boom preventer rigged, to prevent the boom swinging across as the boat rolls; the headsail should be boomed out on the opposite side unless you set a spinnaker or cruising chute in its place.

TACKING

Tacking a big boat is no more difficult than tacking a small one — if anything, it is easier because a cruiser reacts more slowly, giving the helmsman and crew more time to complete their tasks. It does require coordination of effort and correct timing, and all crew members must known their allotted job. Because the sails on a cruiser are so much larger than on a small boat, winches are needed to sheet in the headsail. If you have two crew members, and ordinary as opposed to self-tailing winches, it is best to have one crew member winching while the other tails. If you have self-tailing winches, the job requires only one person, although it will take longer. Before tacking, make sure that you are not pinching the boat, and that it is moving fast. Different designs of boat will vary in the speed at which they tack, so if you are handling a new boat, try it out first in open water. The boat will respond differently in various weather conditions, affected by both wind and waves. The routine shown below works well in most conditions. If you are sailing in stronger winds, or in large waves, you may need to organize the tack more precisely.

How to tack

1 The helmsman, having decided to tack, informs the crew by calling "Ready about". The crew uncleats the sheet without easing it. The helmsman calls "Lee-oh", and pushes the tiller over. The crew releases the sheet.

2 The sails start to move over to the other side of the boat. The crew also moves over to the other side (he should have kept his weight lower than he has here) and begins to haul in the slack on the new jib sheet. The helmsman changes sides, keeping the helm over.

Principles of no go zone

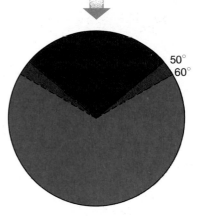

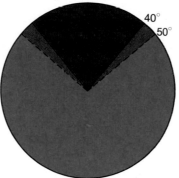

Different boats vary in their ability to sail into the wind. This basically depends on their design and rig. A Marconi sloop-rigged boat will sail a lot closer to the wind than a gaff-rigged boat, and a stream-lined boat will sail much closer to the wind than a family cruiser with smaller sails. Weather conditions will also affect the boat's ability to sail to windward. Whereas you might get the boat to point up to an angle of 40° to the wind in a Force 3 (8 knots), the closest you will get in strong winds – Force 7 (30 knots), for example – will be around 50°. These factors are important on a windward leg of a journey. Tide will also affect the course you can or should sail to windward.

In light to moderate conditions, most modern cruisers will point up to about 40° to 50° to the true wind.

In strong winds and large waves, the pointing angle of all boats will suffer – 50° to 60° may be the best that can be achieved.

3 *The crew puts a couple of turns on the winch and continues to take in the slack on the new jib sheet.*

4 *He then begins to winch in the new headsail sheet. The helmsman can help the crew by slowing down the turn so that the sail does not completely fill on the new side. With a large head-sail rigged, an extra crew member should lift its skirt over the lifelines. The helmsman steers the boat onto the new close-hauled course.*

JIBING

Jibing is the process of altering course away from the wind so that the stern passes through it, and the sails fill on the new side, having swung across the boat. Unlike tacking, the mainsail remains full throughout the jibing maneuver and therefore moves over to the new side faster and with greater force. As a consequence, it is very important to maintain control of the boat throughout the maneuver.

The change of course in jibing is variable unlike when tacking, when there has to be a predetermined degree of course-change in order to pass through the no go zone. In fact, if you are sailing directly downwind you can jibe with virtually no change of course, and may well do so accidentally if you lose concentration. Equally, you can, if you wish, change course by jibing the boat from one reach to another. The boat, in fact, usually sails more slowly on a course directly downwind than it does on a broad reach, and you may find it pays to "tack" downwind, by jibing from one broad reach to another, rather than sailing straight for your objective. In light winds particularly, you should find that the increased speed more than compensates for the greater distance sailed. At its simplest, jibing a cruiser can be less difficult than jibing a small boat, which is inherently less stable.

You will often find, however, that jibing is complicated by the fact that you have been trying to improve the boat's performance. For example, the boat will tend to roll in large waves, and you would normally have rigged a

How to jibe

1 *Put the boat on a broad reach. Check the new course is clear and inform the crew, "Stand by to jibe". The crew makes the new jib sheet ready and has the old one ready to release. He takes up the slack on the new sheet before releasing the old one to prevent the jib from wrapping around the forestay.*

2 *The helmsman steers onto a dead run and sheets in the mainsheet to bring the end of the boom over the quarter, to prevent it sweeping across the boat from one side to the other. (In light winds, of course, this isn't a problem and the helmsman may help the boom's passage by grasping the falls of the mainsheet and pulling on them). The helmsman calls "Jibe-oh".*

boom preventer (see page 69) which you must unrig and re-rig after each jibe. In these conditions you also have to be careful about timing the jibe to prevent a broach. In light or moderate winds, you may try to improve performance by using a spinnaker, a cruising chute or a poled-out headsail to give the boat more driving power. Jibing a spinnaker is not for the inexperienced, and requires practice under the eye of an experienced helmsman (see pages 105–113 for techniques). If you are using a cruising chute, you can jibe it as you would a headsail, provided two sheets are fitted. Otherwise, you will have to lower the chute before the jibe, and reset it afterwards. Similarly, with a poled-out headsail, the pole must be removed before the jibe and reset on the new side afterwards.

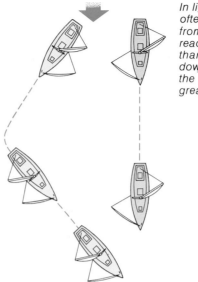

In light winds, it is often faster to jibe from one broad reach to another than to sail directly downwind, although the distance sailed is greater.

3 *The helmsman moves to the new side and changes hands on the tiller. He allows the boat to turn until the sails swing to the new side. As soon as the boom starts to swing he centers the tiller to stop the turn. The crew releases the old sheet and sets the sail on the new side. As the boom swings across, the helmsman controls it with the mainsheet and then lets it swing out to the correct point.*

4 *Once the jibe is accomplished, the helmsman can steer the boat onto the new course and set the sails correctly. The boom preventer, headsail pole and cruising chute, if needed, can be set.*

STEERING THE BOAT

The helmsman's role on a sailing boat is a vital one since he is directly in control of the boat's course and performance. On every cruising boat there should be more than one person capable of steering proficiently on all points of sailing, in both open and congested waters.

On any point of sailing, except close-hauled, the boat's course is determined by the passage plan or chosen heading. Normally the boat is pointed towards the destination, or a land or sea mark en route, or it is steered on an appropriate compass course worked out by the navigator. The helmsman must be able to steer a more or less accurate course (to a tolerance within 5° of the required heading) so that the navigator can then plot the course correctly. Beginners often use too much helm and the boat weaves a rather unsteady course as a result – all helm movements should be kept to the minimum. Steering to a visible mark is easier than steering a compass course (right). When sailing to a windward destination the boat will often have to tack several times and in these circumstances the helmsman should aim to get the best performance out of the boat, rather than steer to a predetermined heading, but he must make a note of the average compass heading he is steering and inform the navigator what it is, and if it changes.

Taking a range

Whenever you are sailing in tidal waters, the movement of the water in relation to the seabed will always affect the course you sail or your boat speed, or both. Most of the time it is the navigator's job to calculate the effect of a tidal stream or current and to plot a course which will allow for it. However, there are times, when sailing in sight of land, when you need to be able to adjust your course by eye to allow for a stream setting across your course. You can do this by finding a range either ahead or astern of the boat. It consists of lining up two fixed points – land or sea marks – and steering the boat to keep them constantly in line. In a cross-stream you will have to point the boat uptide of your objective to keep the objects in line. If you do so, your boat will actually move crab-wise across the seabed, but you will achieve the most direct and the quickest course to your chosen destination.

Steering a compass course

Every boat should have at least one large compass fixed to the cabin bulkhead or some other point where it can be clearly seen by the helmsman from either side of the boat. Most compasses show the course on a card which is marked in degrees, up to 360°, clockwise around its face. To steer a particular course the lubber line in front of the compass must be lined up with the appropriate degree number on the card. If the helmsman is told to steer a particular compass course, he should try to find a land or seamark more or less in line with this course, and then use the mark occasionally as a heading, rather than the compass, so he doesn't strain his eyes from watching the compass continually. Beginners often forget which way to push or pull the tiller to bring the boat back on course if they wander off it. To correct an error, if you want a higher number than the one you are on (say from 110° to 180°) turn the bow of the boat to the right (starboard) by pulling the tiller to the left (port). To go to a lower number (say from 180° to 110°) turn the bow of the boat to the left (port) by pushing the tiller to the right (starboard), until the required number lines up with the lubber line.

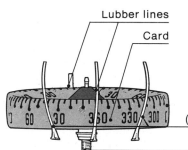

Lubber lines

Card

45° lines (used for side viewing)

Pivot

Compass card mounted on a gimballed frame. The degrees are marked off up to 360°.

The white printed lines on the face of this compass are the main and 45° lubber lines. The center one should be used to read off the heading if the viewer is directly in front of it. The two lubber lines are used if the viewer is seated to one side but the degree number used will be different to the actual heading.

The effects of leeway

Whenever the boat is sailing on or above a beam reach the effect of leeway has to be considered, as under these conditions there will be a certain amount of sideslip as well as forward movement. The result will be that the boat is pushed to leeward of the point at which it is pointing, and this amount of side slip has to be calculated, and taken into consideration in the course steered. When steering for an objective on a course when leeway is present you should aim the boat slightly to windward of your objective to counter the effect of leeway. When sailing out of sight of land, the navigator will have to estimate its likely effect. In most well-designed cruisers you would normally expect leeway of 5° or less when sailing upwind in moderate conditions, possibly increasing to 10° or more in strong winds.

Wind shifts

Although it may appear to be so, the direction and strength of the wind is never constant. Being aware of shifts in the wind and knowing how to use them is vital when sailing close to the wind. Any minor alteration in wind direction will be to your advantage or disadvantage depending on whether it is a "freer" or a "header" (below). A header is a wind shift in which the direction of the wind changes so that it comes from more in front of you. On a close-hauled course, it will prevent you from reaching your objective on one tack. If it is ignored, the boat will stall and slow down, and you will have to bear away to get the sails to fill again. Your course then alters away from your destination and you will have to put in another tack. A freer is a wind shift which has the opposite effect to a header. As you sail along close-hauled, constantly luffing up and bearing away to find the edge of the no go zone, you will find that you will be able to sail closer to your objective than before the wind shift as the no go zone will have moved farther away from you.

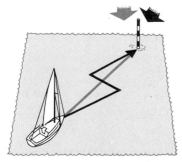

Header

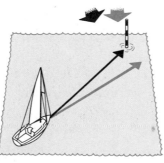

Freer

Apparent wind

The sails always have to be set at the correct angle to the wind, but it may surprise you to know that there is more than one wind: the true or natural wind, and the "apparent wind", a combination of the true wind and the wind created by the movement of the boat. When the boat is sailing with the true wind forward of the beam, the apparent wind will be stronger, and angled farther ahead than the true wind. When the boat is sailing with the true wind aft of the beam, the apparent wind is weaker than the true wind, but still comes from farther ahead except when on a dead run when there is no difference in direction. In practice, the only wind you feel when sailing is the apparent one. However, it can be useful for the navigator to be able to calculate the strength and direction of the true wind, as shown below.

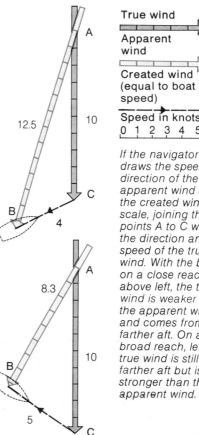

True wind

Apparent wind

Created wind (equal to boat speed)

Speed in knots
0 1 2 3 4 5

If the navigator draws the speed and direction of the apparent wind and the created wind to scale, joining the points A to C will give the direction and speed of the true wind. With the boat on a close reach, above left, the true wind is weaker than the apparent wind, and comes from farther aft. On a broad reach, left, the true wind is still from farther aft but is stronger than the apparent wind.

DOWNWIND SAILING

When sailing downwind in light airs, you may wish to consider ways of improving the boat's performance, as most Marconi-rigged sloops are underpowered on this point of sailing. If you are not sufficiently experienced to handle a spinnaker (see pages 105–113) or if you don't have enough crew on board, then you must consider the other options. These are: poling out a large headsail, flying a cruising chute, or using twin headsails. You will also need to get the mainsail to perform as efficiently as possible, and it should be eased out as much as possible, but not so far that the boom touches the shrouds. If you have a slack boom vang, you will not get a good performance out of the mainsail, as the boom will rise and the mainsail with twist, resulting in loss of power. It may also cause the boat to roll violently in strong winds, and possibly to broach (opposite). To prevent an accidental jibe you can rig a boom preventer (opposite).

Steering on downwind courses is more difficult when there are large waves. If the boat is on a broad reach, the wave crests will pick up the quarter of the boat, and attempt to turn the boat to windward, so the helmsman must steer to counteract this tendency.

Cruising chutes

You can supplement your downwind sailing wardrobe with a cruising chute (a large poleless cruising sail). Unlike the conventional spinnaker, it is an assymetrical sail, set from the spinnaker or headsail halyard and attached by the tack to the bow fitting. As it requires neither pole nor guy, nor sophisticated tackle, it is much simpler to control. Twin sheets are led back from the clew of the sail to the spinnaker winches on either side, outside all the rigging. Set up in this way, the cruising chute can be jibed like a headsail.

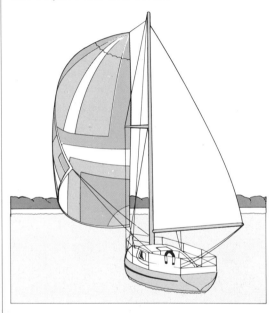

Poling out a headsail

A headsail can be poled out to give extra speed in light weather, or to balance the boat when running downwind in strong winds. A spinnaker pole is normally used, to pole out the sail. Clip the inboard end of the pole to the mast and attach an uphaul/downhaul. Take a spinnaker guy (or a spare long sheet) through a fairlead, well aft, and outside all the rigging, before attaching it to the downhaul fitting on the end of the pole. With the headsail sheeted to leeward, clip the lazy windward headsail sheet into the pole end and raise the pole level with the height of the headsail clew. Position the pole, using the guy, about 50° back from the headstay. Jibe the sail by pulling in the lazy sheet.

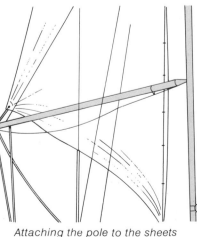

Attaching the pole to the sheets

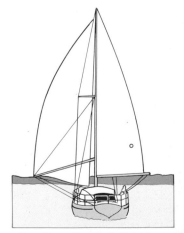

Running wing-and-wing.

Twin headsails

Extra drive can be achieved by hoisting two headsails, with one poled out to windward (below). The technique is also sometimes used offshore on a run, with the mainsail lowered, in order to prevent the mainsail chafing on the shroud. It is best suited to boats with twin headstays, or a twin-grooved headfoil. It can still be used with a single headstay by hoisting two headsails with the hanks of the two sails attached alternately on the headstay, or by setting one of the sails flying.

Above, two headsails hoisted on twin headstays.

Broaching

Broaching is when the boat turns violently to windward, out of control. It is most common when broad reaching or running but can happen on any point of sailing. A common cause of broaching is rolling, which gives the hull an assymetrical underwater shape causing the boat to move in the opposite direction to the way it is heeled. When this force is great enough to overcome the effect of the rudder, the boat will broach. If the mainsail is too large in proportion to the headsail or spinnaker, it will contribute to the tendency to broach, as once the broach has started the mainsail will assist the turn. If a broach occurs, the mainsheet should be eased out immediately and, once the boat is back under control the mainsail area should be reduced.

The yacht, above, has just started to broach while attempting to jibe, probably as a result of sheeting in the mainsail.

Boom preventer

When sailing downwind there is always the danger of an accidental jibe. The best way to prevent this occurring is to rig a boom preventer which fixes the boom on one side of the boat. Once you have rigged the line, ease out the mainsheet until the boom is out slightly too far and then pull in the boom preventer until it is just taut before securing it. The mainsheet is then pulled in to fix the boom in position. To jibe deliberately, you must, of course, remove the boom preventer first, and then fix it in position on the new side after the jibe.

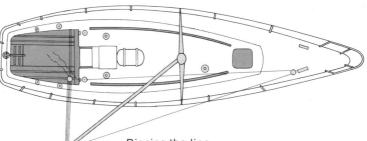

Rigging the line
To rig a boom preventer, attach a line to the end of the boom, preferably with a snap shackle. Lead it forward outside all the rigging and make it fast to a forward deck cleat or lead the line through a forward fairlead and back aft as shown.

CONTROLLING BOAT SPEED

Although most of your sailing time will be spent trying to make the boat go as fast as possible, there will be plenty of occasions when it will be vital to handle the boat competently at slow speeds. Being able to do so, particularly when under sail, and being able to stop under full control, are neglected arts, particularly now that many boats have an engine, and the usual recourse in difficult conditions is to take down the sails and switch it on. However, there will be many times when it may not be practical or convenient to use the engine, and it is reassuring to know that you can handle the boat efficiently without it.

When practicing man-overboard drill, as here, the ability to control boat speed is essential.

Slowing the boat

Obviously the simplest way of reducing speed is to reduce the sail power. On upwind courses above a beam reach, you can ease the sheets so that the sails flap slightly. Speed can then be increased by sheeting in, and reduced by easing out, the sails. For a more permanent slow speed, the sails can be reefed or lowered. On a downwind course, the mainsheet cannot be eased since the boom will be prevented by the shrouds from going out any farther. The jib can be eased sufficiently to spill wind, but this may not be enough; again, the sails can be

reefed, or if the course is not critical, the boat can be turned to a close reach and the mainsail eased. When sailing at slow speeds, the boat may handle quite differently. The steering may feel sluggish and the boat will tend to be more affected by crosswinds, drifting to leeward quite noticeably when slowing down on an upwind heading. Take care that the bow does not blow downwind or the sails will fill again, and the boat will pick up speed.

Using a leadline

There may be occasions when the skipper of the boat asks the crew to check the water depth using a leadline, the traditional method of measuring it. The boat should be sailed slowly forward using the techniques above, and a crew member should be asked to go forward to the leeward shroud with the leadline, which is marked at regular intervals along its length with knots or marks representing fathoms or meters. The lead should be swung forward, and the line let out until the lead hits the seabed. When the leadline is vertical, the user should note the number of knots or the marking at the water's surface, and inform the skipper.

1 *Stand near the shrouds with the coiled leadline in one hand and the end of the line nearest the lead in the other.*

2 *Swing the lead forwards, underarm, and allow the rest of the line to run out until the lead hits the seabed. Take the depth when the line is vertical and the lead is on the bottom.*

Heaving-to

Heaving-to is one of the most important handling techniques. It allows you to stop or slow down the boat under full control. This can be useful if you want to rest the crew for a while, or if the weather is too rough to sail normally. Because of the effect of tidal streams and the boat's windage, the boat will not lie completely stationary but will drift, and the navigator must take this into account. The way in which a boat will lie steadiest depends on the weather conditions and the boat's drifting characteristics. No definite rules can be given about the method to use and the skipper must find what suits his boat in various conditions. For short stops in light airs, let the sails out and lash the tiller to leeward. The boat will then drift slowly to leeward and move ahead as the boat alternately luffs and bears away. However, this method should not be used for long stops, as the flogging of the sails puts a great deal of strain on them and the rigging. For longer stops, back the headsail, ease out the mainsail and lash the tiller to leeward (right and below). This is known as 'heaving-to'. It works best in long-keeled craft; fin-keeled boats may not lie steadily and you will have to experiment with the sail and tiller positions. If you are heaving-to in order to ride out rough weather, you may find it necessary to lower one of the sails to reduce the sail area. Which sail you choose to lower will depend on the design of the boat and you will have to find out by experimenting.

Hove-to, above right and right, with the headsail backed, the mainsail eased, and the tiller lashed to leeward to balance the effect of the backed headsail, the boat will normally lie fairly steadily, moving forwards very slowly while drifting to leeward. Experiment alone will show you how your boat lies when hove-to. In strong winds, a small jib and reefed mainsail or trysail should be used.

CHANGING SAILS

At various times you will have to make the decision to change to a larger or smaller headsail, depending on weather conditions, and the kind of reefing equipment your boat has. Your aim is to keep the boat sailing well and balanced at all times, but not to the point of being over-pressed. The methods of headsail changing depend to some extent on the type of headstay system fitting on your boat. Twin head-foils make the task quicker and boat-handling easier since you can hoist the new sail before lowering the old one, thus always keeping one headsail full. All your sails must be properly bagged up with the tack protruding from the mouth of the sailbag, and the bag marked clearly with the number and name of the sail.

Your crew will find headsail changing easier if the boat is on a downwind course, so that the mainsail blankets the foredeck and the boat doesn't pitch into the waves. The crew should wear harnesses and clip on lifelines while working on the foredeck. Sails should be moved along the foredeck with care, down the windward side-deck, if the weather is too rough for them to be passed through the forehatch.

Changing a headsail

If the boat is fitted with a single headstay system and hanked sails, the old sail will have to be removed before the new sail can be hanked on and hoisted. Although one crew member can do the job, it is quicker and easier with two, one working forward, gathering up the old sail and bending on the new one, and the other dealing with the halyard and sheets. The new sail should be brought up on the foredeck and the bag secured near the bow. The old sail is lowered as described on page 57, and passed back to be bagged and stowed. The halyard should be secured to the pulpit while the new sail is hanked on and the sheets attached. While the foredeck crew hanks on the sail, the other crew member attaches the sheets, adjusts the fairleads, if necessary, and prepares to hoist the sail. If two headstays are fitted (but not so close together that the hanks catch on the other sail) then the new sail can be hoisted before the old one is lowered. However, at least one spare sheet will be needed, and it should be led on the leeward side. When the old sail is lowered, a sheet can be removed and led on the windward side. If the sail is being used again shortly it can be temporarily stowed on the foredeck.

Right, changing a headsail is most quickly carried out by two crew members, one working at the bow while the other tends the halyard and changes the sheets.

Left, when bringing a sail bag on deck, drag it along the windward side-deck.

Below left, lowering the old sail – the crew member is secured by his lifeline so that he has both hands free to work.

Below, after hanking on the new sail, the crew checks that the halyard is not fouled aloft.

EQUIPMENT FOR DOCKING

Your boat is probably going to have to spend a good deal of its life berthed alongside a pier or float. It is therefore crucial to know how to secure it properly to prevent it from moving around and damaging both itself and other craft. You will also need the proper equipment with which to secure it; good-quality lines (see page 150), fenders of a suitable size and shape for your boat that are strong enough to withstand chafe on rough walls, and cleats and fairleads fixed to your boat, sturdily made and securely bolted on. All the equipment should be checked regularly for signs of wear and tear, if you do not wish to find yourself adrift one night in the middle of a gale.

In normal circumstances, you would choose a berth which is sheltered from the full force of wind and waves, but now and again you may have no alternative. Any equipment must be strong enough to withstand considerable pressure. Make sure that any knots you tie will not come undone (see pages 150–55).

Fenders

Fenders are usually made of plastic, although you do see rope ones occasionally. They are hung over the side of the boat, tied to the stanchions or grabrails, and are carefully positioned to prevent the boat from rubbing against the sides of the berth, or another boat. They come in a variety of shapes and sizes to suit the needs of different boats and docking situations. You will need at least four large fenders on board, preferably more. They are, however, bulky and take up a lot of space. Since only the widest part of the boat normally touches the side of the berth, you need position them only where the side of boat and berth meet. If you are docked alongside an uneven pier, you may find it best to hang a fender board (a wooden plank) outside the fenders, to spread the load evenly and to protect the boat.

At least three fenders are needed alongside.

A fender board positioned correctly outside the fenders

Cleats and fairleads

The cleats on your boat should be as large as possible, since the larger the cleat the less wear there is on the line. There should be no sharp edges to it, and every boat should be equipped with at least four deck cleats which can be used for mooring. Bigger boats will need more. If the lines are under great strain, you should have a Samson post (center of picture, right). Your boat should have a fairlead on both sides at the bow and stern so that the lines do not rub against the stanchions or the rigging. The fairleads can be open or closed at the top although the closed type are safer since the line cannot slip out accidentally.

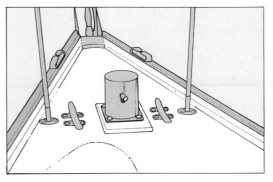

Typical deck layout with cleats, fairleads and Samson post

Docking lines

The lines used for berthing a boat serve different functions. Two lines, known as the bow and stern lines, position the boat correctly in the berth, and are used by the crew to control the boat's speed when coming alongside. The bow and stern lines have to be strong enough to carry the main load of the boat and long enough to allow for any rise and fall of the tide (roughly three times the tidal range). Two other lines, rigged as springs, prevent the boat from moving backwards and forwards, and from rubbing against the side of the berth. These don't need to be as long as the bow and stern lines: one and a half times the tidal range is normally sufficient. The bow and stern lines and the springs need adjusting as the tide rises and falls. The bow and stern lines, provided they are long enough, need only be adjusted at half tide; the springs may need more frequent adjustment. If you are going to leave your boat unattended for some time, you must make sure that you have left enough length on the lines to allow for the tidal range.

When lying alongside a pier or wall do not lead the springs through or under the rails, but take them instead through the fairleads and then outside all the rigging, to prevent chafe on the deck edge or lifelines as the boat rises and falls with the tide. You can use fore and aft breast lines (at the bow and stern) to keep the boat close alongside when loading, for example. They are not, however, essential when both bow and stern lines, and springs, are used. When lying alongside a floating dock they can be used to replace the bow and stern lines. When about to leave a berth, you usually rig the lines ashore as slip lines, so that the crew does not need to go ashore (see page 81).

Below, a boat correctly secured to a floating dock with bow and stern lines, and with springs to prevent any fore-and-aft movement.

Names of lines
All lines used for docking have specific names as shown below.

1 Bow line
2 Stern line
3 Fore breast rope
4 Aft breast rope
5 Fore spring
6 Aft spring

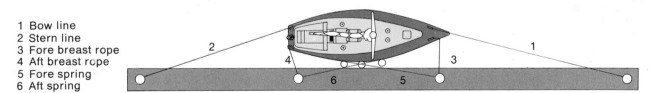

Preventing chafe

No matter how strong your lines, you will find that they chafe against the sides of the boat and the berth unless adequately protected. Since lines are expensive to replace, make sure that you cover the parts likely to get worn with plastic tubing. Although the tension on the line should keep the tubing in place, you can lash it in place with a light line if you prefer.

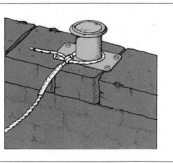

Short length of plastic tubing fixed on a line where it rubs against a rough pier.

DOCKING ALONGSIDE – PREPARATION

Marinas and harbors are often congested and you will probably find it impractical to sail in or out of harbor. Your boat will be under better control if you use power instead.

You may still have to sail in or out of a berth from time to time (possibly without much notice, if your engine fails) and it is an essential part of your seamanship skills to know how to do so. Practice in an uncrowded harbor or marina, where there is plenty of room to maneuver and

to compensate for any errors you may make.

Never make the mistake, even if you are using power, of having your mainsail cover on, the headsails bagged up below decks and the anchor stowed. If anything does go wrong you won't be able to hoist a sail to get yourself out of trouble, and you could drift into another boat or into a pier. Play safe instead by having at least one sail rigged ready for hoisting and the anchor ready to drop, just in case.

Choosing a berth

Although you may not always be able to exercise a great deal of choice in where you dock your boat, there are important considerations to bear in mind when you do. Wherever possible, pick a berth which is sheltered from the wind (having previously listened to the forecast in case any change is likely). You will find a leeward berth (with the dock or pier between you and the wind) much more comfortable than a windward one.

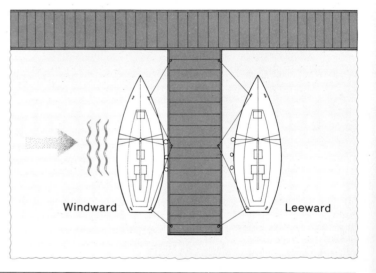

Windward   Leeward

The boat on the windward side of the dock meets the full force of wind and waves, and can get buffeted against the dock. The boat on the leeward side, however, is protected by the dock from the full force of the elements.

Wind and tide effects

The force of the wind and the strength of the tide will have as great an impact as their direction. The design of your boat will determine its reaction to wind effects and you will also have to bear in mind the effects of prop walk on your progress (see pages 54–5). When arriving the main requirement is to get the boat to stop in the right place. If there is no tidal stream, the simplest solution is to approach head-to-wind, using the wind to slow you down. If there is a tidal stream this will often have more effect than the wind, and so you then need to approach the berth head-to-tide if possible.

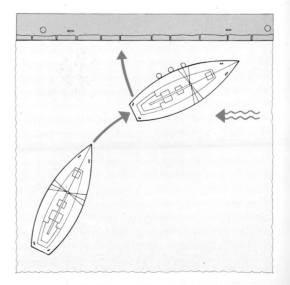

The boat approaching the dock, right, has counter-clockwise prop walk in reverse gear. It is coming in head-to-tide, using the reverse prop walk to bring the stern alongside the dock. If the boat had clockwise prop walk, a shallow angle of approach would be necessary, and the reverse gear would be avoided if possible.

Crew routine

If you are on shore watching a boat docking, you can quickly tell the experienced skipper from the inexperienced. The former accomplishes the maneuver in virtual silence, whereas the latter spends much of the time shouting abuse at the crew. The good skipper briefs his crew in advance, so that they know precisely what is required of them. He also knows their limitations, and does not demand the impossible from them.

It often helps to carry out a dummy run so that the skipper can work out the effects of wind and tide on his approach, and take a look at the mooring points available; the crew get the chance to rig the lines in plenty of time on the appropriate side of the boat, and to get the fenders ready.

Although the routine may vary according to the situation, there is a standard procedure which can usually be followed when coming alongside, with a crew of two in addition to the skipper.

The lines should be prepared with a bow line fixed to the bow cleat, and a stern line to the stern, led through the fairleads and outside all the rigging. The fenders should be attached to the stanchions or lifelines using a round turn and two half hitches (see page 152), where required. The crew then each take a bow and stern line, and stand outside the lifelines near the shrouds holding the coiled lines. As soon as the boat closes with the dock, the crew step ashore. The crew member with the stern line makes it fast aft of the boat by either dropping a bowline over a cleat or taking a turn around whatever fitting is available. The skipper, or any other crew member on board, takes up the slack and, keeping a turn around the stern cleat, lets out the line gradually to slow the boat down, if necessary. The crew member with the bow line makes it fast ashore well ahead of the boat. The two lines are then adjusted to get the boat properly in position in the berth. Any excess line should be coiled on board. Once the bow and stern lines have been secured, you can rig the springs (as shown on page 77). The fore spring runs from a stern cleat, through the appropriate fairlead, outside all the rigging to a point on the pier or dock level with the bow. The aft spring is led similarly from the bow to a point level with the stern. On a short-handed boat it may help to rig an aft spring first midway along the boat. The boat can be held on this, parallel with the pier or dock, while the bow and stern lines are taken ashore and secured.

Left, the crew are correctly positioned outside the life-lines at the shrouds, holding the ready coiled bow and stern lines, so that they can step ashore and fasten the lines rapidly.

Right, a crew member taking a turn around a cleat to hold the boat. Once the boat has been positioned, the lines should be adjusted so that any surplus is coiled on board the boat, not on the dock.

LEAVING AND ARRIVING ALONGSIDE

In the majority of berthing situations you will be trying to bring your boat alongside a pier or floating dock or trying to leave from one when you set off. Unfortunately, there are no rigid rules that will ensure success, because so much depends on the strength and direction of the wind and tide, and the handling ability of your boat under sail or under power. Unless you are a very experienced skipper you would be wise not to attempt arriving at or leaving a tricky berth under sail.

Although there are no hard-and-fast rules, there are a number of situations which you will certainly face at some time, and suitable methods for dealing with them are given on the following pages. As a general rule, however, you will need to face your boat into the strongest element when leaving or returning, and you will find it better under difficult conditions to rig slip lines (opposite) or turn your boat around in the berth using lines and following the method shown opposite, below.

Before attempting to get in or out of a berth you must know how your boat responds under engine, and the direction of the prop walk, both in forward and reverse gear (see page 50). Handling your boat in harbor is a skill which you will learn gradually with practice and experience, and you should have an experienced skipper on board to advise you at first.

Below, coming alongside a float – the crew is about to rig the bow line.

Slip lines

A slip line, as its name implies, is one that can be cast off from on board the boat without undoing a knot on shore. Normally, in berthing, it is led ashore through a ring, or around a bollard or cleat, and then brought back on board. Its main use is for the time when you want to be able to release a line without having to go ashore. For example, if you were berthed alongside a high pier, your crew might otherwise have to make a perilous leap to get on board as you move off.

It is vital, however, to make sure that the line really will slip, and will not catch on its mooring on shore. If you secure the slip through a ring, make sure the end to be released is led up through the ring, if the ring is on top of a wall, or, down through the ring if the ring is on the vertical face of wall. Pull the line steadily without jerking to release it from the ring, and then get it on board quickly before it can foul your propeller.

Above, crew about to release the slip line as the boat leaves an alongside berth.

Turning under lines

You may find that you are berthed in such a way that it is going to be difficult to leave, if the wind or tide is blowing or running in the wrong direction. The solution is to turn the boat around in its berth using lines, so that it is facing in the direction you want to leave from. You will find it easier to move first the end of the boat facing into the strongest element, wind or tide. In the diagrams, below, the boat is facing into the wind, and the skipper wants to leave with the boat facing into the tide. In this case the effect of the wind on the boat is greater than the tide, so he rigs the lines to move the bow away from the pier first.

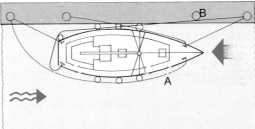

1 *Rig a new line (A) from bow to shore, astern of the boat, outside all the rigging. Lead the existing fore spring (B) similarly from the shore around the stern and cleat it on the outside quarter.*

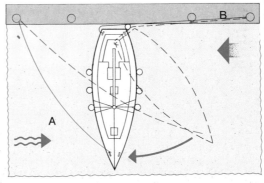

2 *Release all other lines. Pull on B to start the boat turning. Pull on A, or take up the slack on it, until boat lies against quay. At the middle of the turn the boat will swing quickly but will slow down before it comes parallel with the quay.*

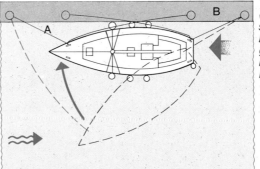

3 *Make fast the new bow and stern lines (A and B). If you are not going to leave immediately, rig new springs.*

Springing off under power

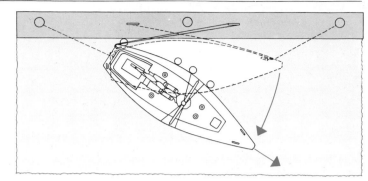

If you were to cast off all your lines, put your engine into forward gear and steer away from the alongside berth, the boat's stern would, in all probability, crash into the side. To avoid this, you need to turn one end of the boat away from the berth before you motor off. In lightweight craft, a crew member can simply push off with a boat-hook, but in larger boats you will need to use springs. Nearly all the methods for leaving under power are based on the principle of springing off, either bow or stern first, depending on the situation (see below). You should put a fender at the bow or stern, as appropriate, to protect it from the pier. Whether you rig the bow or stern line as the spring depends on the direction in which you are leaving. It should be rigged as a slip, so that it can be released from the boat.

Leaving bow first
Rig the fore spring as a slip line, and cast off the other lines. Motor gently astern and turn the *stern towards the wall as the boat starts to pivot. Once clear, release the spring.*

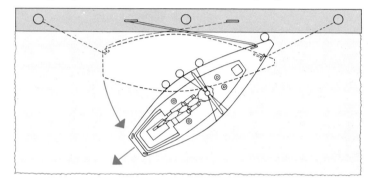

Leaving stern first
Rig the aft spring as a slip line, and cast off the other lines. Motor gently forward and turn *the stern away from the wall. When turned sufficiently, release the spring and motor out astern.*

How to leave

The strongest element, wind or tide, and its direction will determine which way you leave, whether bow or stern first. The methods you use when the tide is the determining factor are shown right. If the wind is not coming from the direction of the sectors shown below right, use either method. If it is blowing strongly offshore, you could leave by simply releasing the lines and drifting away. Obviously this is less controlled than springing off, and if your boat has a lot of windage the bow will blow downwind faster than the stern.

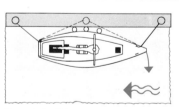

Bow into tide
Leave bow first.

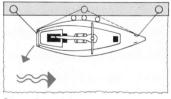

Stern into tide
Leave stern first.

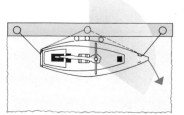

Wind forward of the beam
Leave bow first.

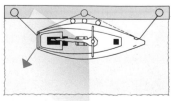

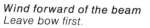

Wind aft of the beam
Leave stern first.

Leaving under sail

You can leave a berth under sail in most conditions, unless the wind is a great deal weaker than the tide, in which case you won't have much control, and it would be wiser to use the engine or to warp the boat out. Generally, it is best to leave bow-to-tide as this will give you more control over the steering and makes stopping much easier. If the boat is berthed stern-to-tide, turn it around as shown on page 81. Having got your boat around to face the tide, the next step is to decide where the wind is coming from and which method, therefore, to use. Whichever method you use, follow the same principles as when under power and cast off last the lines under most strain, using fenders to protect the appropriate corners of the boat. An onshore wind presents problems as the boat will blow onto the quay. Either try and get a tow from a boat with an engine or, alternatively, warp your boat around to a different berth (if there is one). Failing these, lay the anchor using the dinghy (see page 100) at a point some distance upwind. Then row back to the boat, and haul on the anchor line to get the boat away from the wall and in a position to sail off from the anchor. If you arrive at a berth with an onshore wind blowing, and you know you will be leaving shortly, consider dropping the anchor first.
if the wind is offshore and far enough forward of the beam to prevent the mainsail filling, hoist the mainsail first and delay hoisting the headsail until all the lines have been cleared from the foredeck. If the wind is on or aft of the beam, leave under headsail alone, and hoist the main once you are under way.

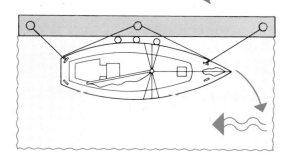

Offshore wind ahead of beam
Hoist the mainsail. Release the shore lines. Once the boat has drifted clear, trim the mainsail, hoist and trim the headsail.

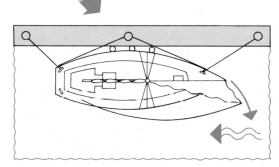

Offshore wind aft of beam
Hoist the headsail. Cast off the lines and trim the headsail. Once clear, turn head-to-wind to hoist the mainsail.

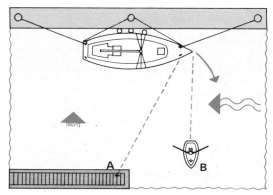

Onshore wind
The boat can either be warped off by attaching a line to the jetty (A) or by laying an anchor (B).

Leaving a berth under headsail alone

Arriving under power

When approaching a berth under power you should follow the guidelines already set down on page 80, making a dummy run if necessary to assess the relative strength of the wind and tide. Before making the final approach your lines should be cleated on board and led outside the lifelines and shrouds, your fenders tied on and lowered, and your crew properly briefed as to your intentions. In certain situations, you will be able to use the prop walk of your engine to help you berth. If you have sailed into the harbor, switch your engine on and allow it time to warm up before attempting to berth. Give your crew time to get the sails down and loosely furled.

Coming into an alongside berth – the crew are getting ready to step ashore with the bow and stern lines.

How to arrive

If the wind and tide are parallel to the shore, whether from the same direction or opposed, a similar approach is used, right. Come in to the berth with the bow towards the stronger element. Prepare the lines in the usual way and put the engine into neutral when you want the boat to slow down. If the wind and tide are opposed, you may need to use reverse gear as you bring the boat up to the pier.

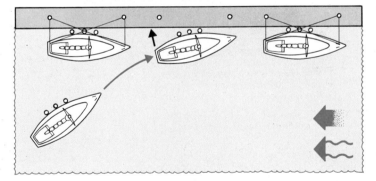

If the wind is onshore the boat should be stopped parallel to and clear of the pier. The wind will then cause it to drift gently sideways into the berth.
With an offshore wind blowing, right, you need to take account of the windage on the bow, as it may push it out away from the pier. Get the crew to lead the stern line well forward and motor into the berth at a sharper angle than usual. Tell the crew to get the bow and stern lines ashore rapidly and pull the boat into position using the lines.

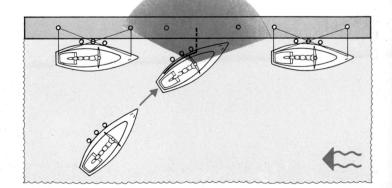

Arriving under sail

Berthing under sail in a crowded harbor is best left to the experts, unless your engine breaks down and you have no choice. You should, however, practice the skills whenever possible. Pick a day with medium-strength winds and keep your engine running in case you get into difficulties. In a harbor you may have the additional problem of wind deflections from high buildings. Most experienced skippers have an escape route worked out in advance – it requires a lot of skill to handle a boat slowly under sail. If you find you are travelling too fast, either partially lower the headsail or get the crew to back the mainsail or jib (by physically holding the mainsail out against the shrouds and the jib out by the leech). The same basic principles apply as when approaching under power.

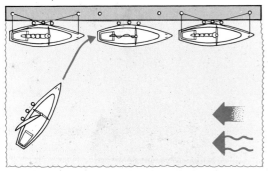

Wind and tide together or strong wind opposed
With wind and tide together, or opposed but with a much stronger wind, approach the berth under mainsail alone on a close reach, letting out the mainsheet as necessary to control boat speed. As you reach the berth, turn the boat into the wind, and back the mainsail if necessary to slow down in the final stages. Once alongside, fasten the bow and stern lines ashore and drop and furl the mainsail quickly.

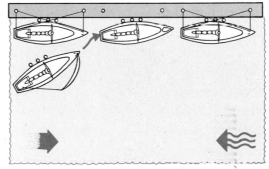

Strong tide opposing weak wind
With the tide stronger than, and opposed to, the wind, approach downwind under headsail alone. Keep the sail sheeted in lightly, and if the approach is too fast, lower the headsail a little and get a crew member to hold the leech out, or take the sail down altogether and make the final approach under bare poles. Get the stern line and an aft spring ashore first and secure them to act as a brake.

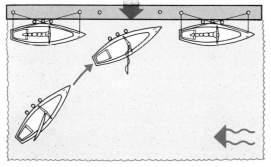

Offshore wind
With the wind blowing offshore, come in against the tide. If the wind is forward of the beam, come in under the mainsail, and if it is aft of the beam, come in under the headsail. Sail into the berth, and adjust the speed by letting out the sheet. Get the bow and stern lines ashore quickly but don't pull in the stern until the mainsail is lowered. (The diagram above shows the approach under mainsail alone.)

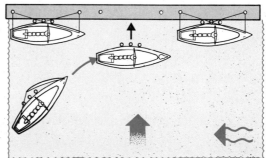

Onshore wind
When the wind is blowing onto the berth, make the approach under headsail alone. Lower the mainsail to windward of the berth and sail downwind under the headsail. About a boat's length to windward of the berth, turn the boat almost parallel with the pier, with the bow pointing slightly upwind. Lower the sail (or allow it to flap) and let the boat drift sideways into the berth. Fasten the bow and stern lines.

RAFTING UP

Rafting up is the term given to berthing along-side another boat. In crowded harbors you may have no choice but to raft up if you are making an overnight stop, for example, although it is not the ideal berthing arrangement. More often than not several boats are rafted up together, and if you happen to be on the inside of the raft and wish to leave first, getting out is not easy (opposite). Most harbors limit the number of boats that can raft up together, so try to find out what the rules are first. Always ask permission of the boat you are rafting up to,

simply out of politeness. If you are the outside boat on a raft of several, your lines must be long enough to reach the shore, otherwise you may have to drop anchors fore and aft. Avoid a raft with only the inside boat made fast to the shore if you do not wish your boat to swing uncomfortably to and fro. It is best to raft up alongside a boat larger than your own, with the masts staggered so that the rigging doesn't foul if the boats roll. When coming ashore, walk forward of the masts of the other boats in the raft – it helps preserve their privacy.

Joining a raft

There is no need to face in the same direction as the other boats when joining a raft. If anything, it helps to face the other way so the masts do not get tangled. Check that all of the boats have lines fastened to the shore, as well as to the other boat, or boats, and make sure your own lines are long enough to reach the shore. Follow the usual procedure for approaching an alongside berth.

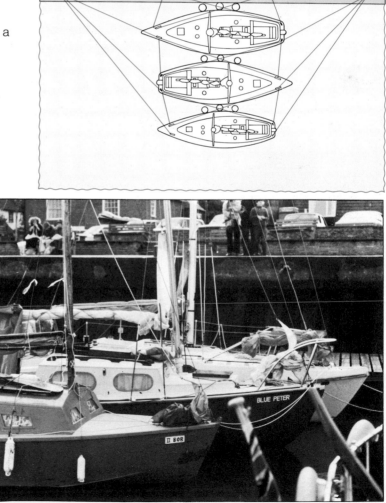

Above right, boats correctly rafted up with the breast lines and springs rigged in the usual way, but attached to cleats on the neighboring boat. The bow and stern lines are rigged to the shore, outside the lines of the other boats.

Right, boats rafted up to a float with the smallest boat on the outside. However, it has only fore and aft breast lines, whereas it should also have bow and stern shore lines rigged.

Leaving a raft

When leaving a raft, provided you are on the outside, you can operate in the same way as you would for an alongside berth. If you leave from the middle of the raft, your exit needs more careful consideration. You must leave with the strongest element so the boats outside will drift back together. If you leave against the strongest element, they will drift out, leaving you with a knotty problem to solve.

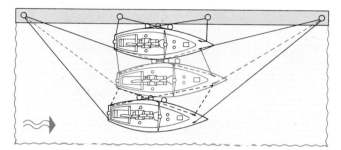

1 *Unfasten your bow and stern lines and springs, and bring them on board. Unfasten the springs and breast ropes of the boat outside you.*

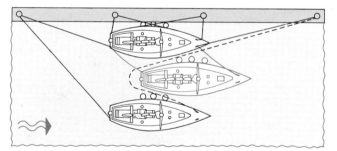

2 *Unfasten your bow and stern lines and springs, and bring them on board. Unfasten the springs and breast lines of the boat outside you.*

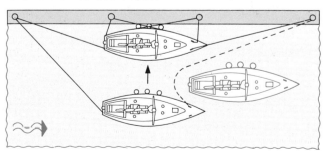

3 *Let go of the breast lines of your own boat and allow it to move out with the strongest element. If your crew are still on the raft, turn and come alongside the outside boat in the raft to pick them up.*

A long raft at a popular harbor during the sailing season.

Rafting up around a mooring buoy

You may find a harbor with several large mooring buoys around which boats have moored up, bow-on, and rafted together. This arrangement is only suitable for use in non-tidal waters. When you arrive you should make fast to the buoy first, then use springs and breast lines to secure your boat to the neighboring one. When you leave, take in your springs and breast lines, untie from the buoy and leave stern first. If the other boats are unattended, you may need to leave a crew member aboard one boat to secure the lines. He is then picked up from an outside boat as you leave the raft.

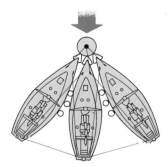

Boats rafted up around a mooring buoy

MARINA BERTHS

Marinas provide a number of floating docks in a small area (right), often with good amenities ashore. As a result, they are becoming increasingly popular. However, the berths are very close together and the marina can get uncomfortably crowded in season. You must therefore be able to control your boat in congested waters if you are not to cause havoc.

Some marina harbor masters stipulate that boats should arrive and leave under power as space to maneuver is limited. There will be occasions when you can berth or leave only by making a three-point turn, and it helps if your boat handles well in reverse gear. It would be foolhardy to try to berth the boat in a confined space if it has a lot of windage and a weak engine. Your recourse would be to come alongside an outside berth and warp the boat around to the confined berth afterwards.

Among the many advantages that marinas offer are the facilities of shops and showers close at hand, and the fact that most of them are located out of the tidal stream.

The same general principles apply to marinas as to alongside berthing situations.

Handling a difficult berth

In some berths you may find that your room to maneuver is so limited that you have no choice but to warp your boat in or out of the berth. This means using the lines attached to the boat to lead it into or out of the berth, rather in the manner that bargemen used to control their canal boats. It isn't possible, unfortunately, to lay down hard-and-fast rules – you have to use common sense and work out for yourself the most logical method. A point to remember is that it is usually easy to start the boat moving using lines, and rather harder to stop it once it has started! An alternative solution to warping the boat is to use a spring and the engine to get the boat out of the berth, particularly when reversing out of a confined space or when a strong wind is blowing.

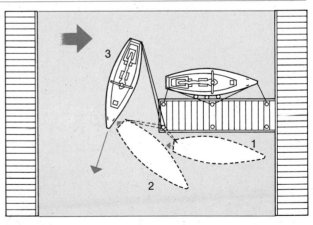

The boat, above, has limited turning room, and a strong wind is blowing, which could prevent the bow of the boat from going up to windward. If the stern line is rigged as a slip line, the boat can be motored out astern, leaving slack on the line (1). Once the stern is clear of the berth (2), a turn can be taken on the cleat to hold the stern until the bow can clear the berth (3), and then the line can be freed and allowed to slip as the boat motors forward into clear water.

Leaving

Before leaving a marina berth, you should have a good look around to establish the best method of leaving. It is important to check whether any other boats are in the process of docking or leaving, lest they interfere with your chosen course. The next step is to consider the effects of wind (and tide, if there is any) and your path out of the marina. You will have to move out at slow speed. Don't forget the basic rule of keeping to the right of the fairway once you are in open water. If a boat is approaching you, and is clearly less maneuverable than your own, common sense dictates that you get out of the way.

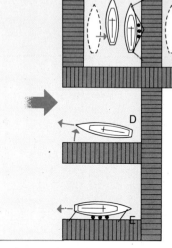

If you have a simple berth to leave from (A and B), put the engine in neutral before the lines are cast off, then let the boat drift clear of the berth.

Motor into open water. If there isn't enough wind to take the boat clear, push the bows off. Berth C is more difficult, as the boat is bow-on in a windward berth. Either spring off the stern (1), or warp the boat out (2), so it can leave bow-to-wind. With berth D, you can motor straight out if the bow is pushed off. With berth E, you can reverse straight out if the boat has a clockwise prop walk in reverse. Otherwise the crew could warp the boat out using the stern line and aft spring, coming aboard when it reaches the end of the dock.

Arriving

As a visitor to a marina you should first try to find out what the regulations are, and where you are permitted to berth your boat. If in doubt, tie up at an outside berth and go along to the harbor master's office to inquire. As you may not be able to see where you are docking until just before you approach the berth, the crew must be able to respond quickly to your instructions. You may find it helps, provided you have enough, to rig lines and fenders on both sides of the boat. Watch out for any other boats entering or leaving the marina and give way to less maneuverable craft. If you have any choice of berth, take one where you can put the boat head-to-wind, so that drafts don't blow through the cabin.

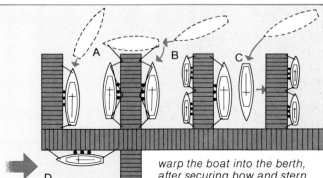

If your boat has little prop walk, come in stern first (A), allowing the stern to lie slightly upwind of the berth. If your boat is less easy to maneuver (B), bring the boat alongside the end of the dock head-to-wind and

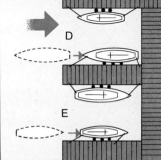

warp the boat into the berth, after securing bow and stern lines. On a windward dock (C), berth bow first, approaching in neutral, and allow the wind to do the work. With good control in reverse (D), come in stern first using forward gear to stop. With less control in reverse (E), come in bow first. Get a crew member to jump ashore quickly and to secure the aft spring and stern line to help slow the boat down as you come in. Rig all the lines in the usual way.

Berthing stern-to

In some marinas, particularly around the Mediterranean, the boats have to be berthed stern-to and secured at the bow with an anchor, so that the boat lies at right angles to the dock. You therefore need to know how to anchor your boat (see pages 96–103). The berths are easier to leave from than to return to, unless your boat happens to have good handling characteristics in reverse gear. If you have to berth your boat regularly in this type of marina, it is worth making an opening in the stern rail and keeping a gangplank aboard, to make access easier. The boat needs little in the way of mooring lines – simply a couple at the stern rigged like the usual springs.

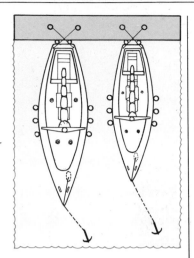

Leaving

When leaving a stern-to berth, the routine is virtually the same whatever the direction of wind or tide. The stern lines are released and the boat motored forward while the anchor cable is recovered. Once the boat is over the anchor, the anchor is broken out and the boat taken clear of the berth. With a strong cross-wind or tide it is best to rig a stern line as a slip. The crew controls any sideways movement by pulling on the stern line and the anchor line. The stern line can be slipped once the anchor is broken out.

Arriving

Get the crew to rig the fenders over the stern and the sides of the boat if necessary. Lay the anchor in the usual way (see pages 96–103) and then reverse slowly into the berth while a crew member pays out the anchor cable. In a cross-wind, the anchor should be laid upwind of the berth (right). If the boat swings out of line, get the crew to snub the anchor cable briefly. Once you reach the dock, the crew should rig the stern lines in the usual way, so that the boat lies just clear of the berth. If there is a strong cross-wind you may find it better to motor in bow first, attach a line to the shore and reverse out, paying out the line until you reach the anchoring position. Then lay the anchor, take the slack line to the stern and reverse into the berth, berthing stern-to in the usual way.

Right, in strong cross-winds and with a weak engine, it may help to work in two stages. In the first stage, right, motor into the berth bow first (1), and fasten a bow line ashore (2) before reversing out, paying out the bow line as you go, and lay anchor (3). In the second stage, far right, turn the boat on the anchor (4), untie the bow line and attach it to the stern; then reverse into the berth using the anchor rode and new stern line as a guide (5). Fasten the stern springs to the shore (6).

Motor in parallel to the berth clear of any lines (1), lay the anchor (2), and reverse into the berth (3). Attach the stern springs in the usual way. With a cross-wind blowing, the anchor should be laid upwind to hold the boat steady in the berth.

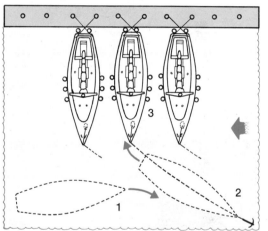

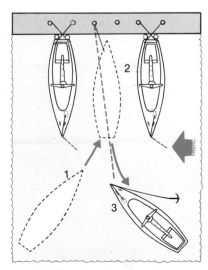

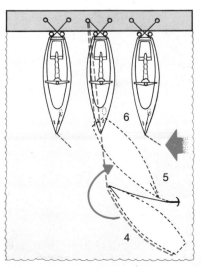

Pile and float berths

Some marinas have a system whereby pairs of piles are used to secure the boat at right angles to the float. This avoids having to lay the anchor, as you can attach the stern or bow of the boat to the piles. If you have a permanent berth, rig permanent lines to the piles and to the float so that leaving and arriving is made easier, as you only have to pick up the rigged lines. If no permanent lines are laid, however, you will have to use your own lines to attach the boat to the piles and the float, and remove them as you leave. If your boat has a weak engine, berth bow-on, rather than reversing in. In such berthing situations, a long or telescopic boat-hook can be very useful to allow you to reach the piles easily.

Arriving

If there are no permanent lines fixed to the piles and the float, the crew should rig two bow lines and two stern lines. The ends of the stern lines should be led forward to the shrouds. Motor in bow-on and stop with the shrouds alongside the upwind or uptide pile. Attach the stern line, then allow the boat to drift downwind or downtide to the other pile. Attach that stern line and then motor into the berth and attach the bow lines. If permanent lines are rigged from the piles, they can simply be picked up with a boat-hook as you motor in.

Leaving

The instructions on this page are for berthing a boat bow-on. If you wish to lie stern-first, then simply reverse the instructions for bow and stern. If permanent lines are rigged, ignore the instructions for rigging the lines.

The method you use will depend on the direction of the wind. If it is from ahead or astern, your task is simpler. Rig your stern lines as slip lines and take them forward to the shrouds. Then cast the bow lines off and pull the boat back through the piles using the stern slips. As your boat comes level with the piles, release the slip lines.

With a strong cross-wind blowing, you will have to pull the boat up to the windward pile so that you don't drift onto the leeward pile as you depart. Ease out the windward bow and stern lines and let the boat drift across to the leeward pile. Release the leeward stern and bow lines, and pull the boat back up to windward using the windward lines. Rig an extra line as a slip from the windward pile to a point near the bow. Then release the bow and stern lines and motor the boat out astern. If you find the bow drifting to leeward a little, tighten the slip line briefly to pull the bow back up to windward. Once you are clear of the piles you can slip the line.

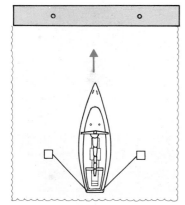

1 *Rig stern and bow lines. Bring stern lines to shrouds and attach the ends to piles.*

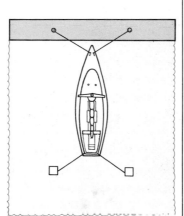

2 *Motor forward, paying out stern lines, and fasten bow lines to float.*

Cross-winds

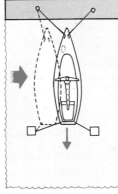

1 *Ease windward bow and stern lines to release leeward lines.*

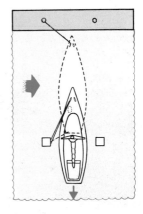

2 *Rig slip line from bow to windward pile. Reverse out using it to guide you.*

PILE MOORINGS

Wooden or metal stakes driven into the seabed, known as piles, are often used as fore and aft moorings along the edge of a channel. They are equipped with sliding ring fittings to which the boat's lines can be attached. In crowded harbors, several boats may raft up to one set of piles, although most harbor masters set limits to the number of boats that can be rafted up together. If you are leaving the boat for any length of time, make sure it is moored up facing into the ebb tide, which is usually stronger than the flood.

Piles are often a convenient form of berthing in a tidal channel, since the ring on the pile slides up and down, which means you do not have to adjust your lines with the rise and fall of the tide. A retrieval line runs from the ring to the top of the pile so that it can be easily reached.

The stern line of this cruiser has just been made fast to the pile, and cleated on deck. The remainder is being coiled neatly by the crew.

Leaving under power

Your method of leaving a pile mooring will depend on whether you are lying alongside another boat, in the middle of a raft, or on your own. If in the middle of a raft, use the methods already described on page 87. If you are on the outside, you can recover your lines in the dinghy, and leave using the methods for an alongside berth already described on pages 80-85. If the boat is on its own between piles, use one of the three methods described below, depending on the strength and direction of the wind and tide, and how your boat handles in reverse gear.

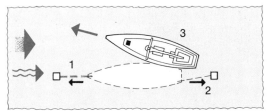

Row into strongest element
Pull the boat forward to the forward pile while paying out on the stern line (1). Rig the bow line as a slip and allow the boat to drop back to the aft pile (2). Release the stern line and motor away forwards as you slip the bow line (3).

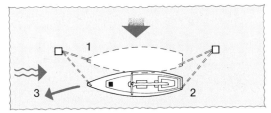

Wind beam
If the bow is pointing into the tide, rig both bow and stern lines as slips (1) and allow the boat to drift to leeward of the piles by slackening the lines and steering away (2). Once clear, slip both lines and motor off forward (3). If the boat is stern-to-tide, see below.

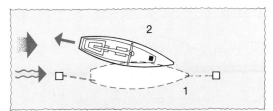

Stern into strongest element
If the boat handles well in reverse, rig both lines as slips (1) and motor out astern (2), preferably in the direction favored by the prop walk. If the boat does not handle well in reverse, turn the boat by using lines (see page 81) and leave using the methods for bow into the strongest element.

Arriving under power

When planning to pick up a pile mooring, the same factors need to be taken into account as when approaching any other berth. You have to work out a course of action according to the relative effects of wind and tide, and the boat's handling characteristics. The bow and stern lines should be made ready, and the fenders lowered; the crew should stand by with a boat-hook to pick up the mooring ring. It will be easier if two crew members cooperate to secure the boat to the pile ring, as one person can hold the boat in position while the other ties the line to the ring (right). If there are other boats alongside the piles, you can use the techniques already described for rafting up on page 86. If staying long, you may need to turn the boat so that it points into the ebb tide.

Wind and tide together
Approach into the wind and tide and stop with the bow alongside the forward pile and attach the bow line (1). Pay out the line to allow the boat to drop back to the aft pile and secure the stern line (2). Pull the boat forwards until it is equidistant from the two piles and adjust the lines. Alternatively, the stern line could be taken to the pile in the dinghy, or the method for wind and tide opposed could be used.

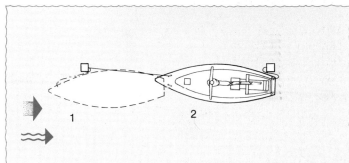

Wind and tide opposed
Approach into the strongest element. Stop at the aft pile first and attach the stern line, but keep it slack (1). Motor forwards to the forward pile and attach the bow line (2). Drop back and adjust the lines to position the boat. It is important that a crew member is delegated to tend the stern line throughout the maneuver to prevent it fouling the propeller. This method is known as a "running moor".

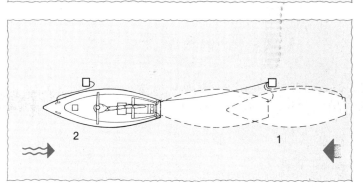

Wind abeam
The method is basically the same as the running moor described above, but the boat approaches the aft pile from the windward side (1). After securing the stern line, motor slowly forward, keeping the bow pointing slightly into the wind so that the boat moves crabwise to the forward pile. Secure the bow line (2) and center the boat in between the two piles.

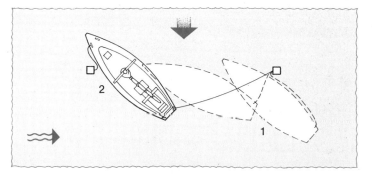

Leaving under sail

Pile moorings are no more difficult to leave from under sail than alongside berths, but as with all other berthing maneuvers, it is best not to make the attempt if the area is crowded, unless you have no choice. Pile moorings are normally sited on the edge of a channel, in the tidal stream, and so you should normally leave bow-to-tide, as this gives you better control over your speed and steering when under sail. You may have to turn the boat first using lines, so that it is facing in the right direction. If yours is the only boat moored up to the piles, use one of the methods shown below. If you are moored up on the outside of a raft of boats, recover your lines rigged to the piles using the dinghy, and then leave using the appropriate methods for alongside berths shown on pages 82–83. If you are unfortunate enough to be in the middle of the raft, you will probably have to persuade the outside boats to cast off so that you can leave, although it may be possible for the experienced sailor to sail or warp out, if no engine power is available.

Fore and aft buoys

In some harbors and estuaries you will find fore and aft buoys rather than piles. You can secure the boat to them at bow and stern, which prevents it swinging in the wind or tide. The methods you use for leaving and approaching are the same as for pile moorings. Before picking up fore and aft buoys, you should check that the moorings are of a sufficient size and weight to secure the boat.

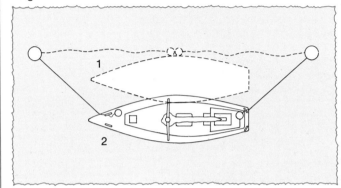

Pick-up buoys
Sometimes the main buoys will have smaller pick-up buoys attached to them by a rope or chain. These are easily picked up and secured on board when mooring up.

When you approach such a berth (above), pick up the buoys together (1) and bring them on board, taking the forward one to the bow and the aft one to the stern (2).

Wind forward of beam
Turn the boat bow-to-tide and prepare both sails for immediate hoisting. Rig the bow and stern lines as slips and keep the stern line slack. Hoist the mainsail (1). Sheet in and steer onto your chosen course, preferably to leeward of the forward pile. Slip the stern line as the boat gathers way, and then slip the bow line (2). Once clear, hoist the headsail.

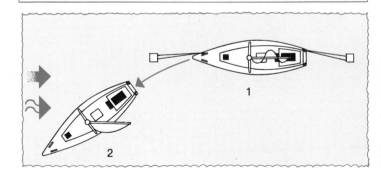

Wind on or aft of beam
Turn the boat bow-to-tide and prepare both sails for hoisting. Rig both lines as slips and hoist the headsail (1). Sheet in the sail, slip the lines and steer onto your chosen course as the boat gathers way (2). As soon as you are clear, turn head-to-wind and hoist the mainsail.

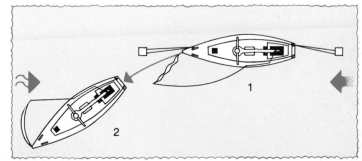

Arriving under sail

When planning to pick up a pile mooring under sail, you must bear in mind the strength of wind and tide when choosing your approach. It is normally best to head the boat into the tide, unless there is a much stronger opposing wind. Whether you use the mainsail or the headsail will depend on the direction of the wind, fore or aft of the beam, as you approach. Your approach has got to be very controlled and slow, so you need to adjust your speed by letting out the sheet of the headsail or mainsail, as appropriate. Your aim is to secure the boat to the upwind pile first, stopping so that it is just by the shrouds. It is important to secure the line immediately and if your crew cannot be relied upon to tie a knot quickly, it is best to rig the lines as slips and hold the boat on those until they can tie the knots at more leisure.

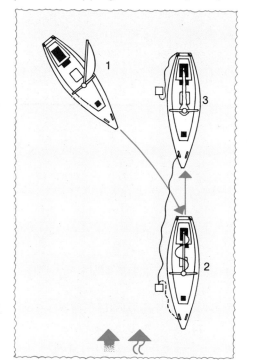

Wind forward of beam
When approaching against the tide with the wind forward of the beam, or into a stronger wind with an opposing weak tide or no tide, approach the forward pile under the mainsail only on a close reach (1). Stop the boat with the pile near the shrouds and secure the bow line (2). Lower the mainsail and allow the boat to drop back to the aft pile and secure the stern line (3). Adjust the lines.

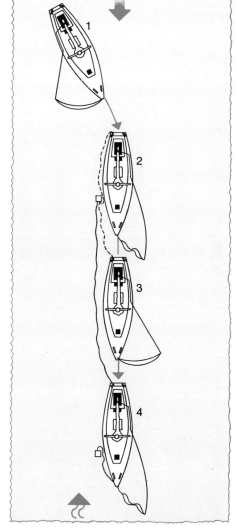

Wind on or aft of beam
When a relatively strong tide is opposing a weak wind, approach into the tide under the headsail alone and use a running moor. After lowering the mainsail, sail towards the aft pile under the headsail (1). Stop by allowing the sail to flap or lowering it partially or totally when the pile is near the shrouds and attach the stern line (2). Then sheet in the sail and approach the forward pile while letting out the stern line (3). Stop the boat against the forward pile and secure the bow line (4). Lower the headsail and adjust the lines so that the boat is positioned equidistant from both of the piles.

ANCHORING AND MOORING

The techniques for anchoring and mooring both involve securing the boat to the bottom with a line. A mooring is fixed permanently to the bottom, but in anchoring you have to do the fixing yourself. It therefore involves extra equipment and more work on the part of the crew, and it involves the skipper in choosing a suitable anchoring ground and it is important that he knows what size and type of anchor to use in different conditions. Quite a few harbors have an area outside the harbor walls, protected from the worst of the weather, which can be used as an anchorage. Your chart or pilot book will give you the necessary information. Moorings, being fixed, are paid for, and if you moor temporarily you should find out first from the harbor master whether you may do so. The actual moorings themselves differ in the size and weight of boat they can safely hold. Sometimes the size of boat a mooring will hold is marked on the buoy.

Boats moored up in an estuary

Anchoring gear

You must have appropriate anchoring equipment on board for your size and type of boat, and you should seek an anchor manufacturer's advice as to the exact weight of anchor you should carry. There are a number of different types designed to suit various holding conditions (see opposite). You will also need anchor rode (right); many craft have a fitting known as a bow roller through which the anchor chain can run. If you use chain rather than rope cable you should have a securely mounted central bollard around which it can be made fast. There are a number of ways the anchor can be stowed: on chocks on the foredeck, on the pulpit, on the bow roller or in a self-draining well. Chain is normally kept in a special chain locker below decks, and is then fed through a pipe on to the foredeck. A windlass is useful for taking the strain out of weighing anchor – the type with twin drums (or gypsies) can be used for both chain and rope cable.

Top right, an anchor stowed on the pulpit; center right a self-stowing anchor on a bow-roller; right, a hand-operated windlass.

Scope

The amount of rode (known as the scope) that you need depends on a number of factors: the type of rode (whether line, chain or a mixture of the two), the depth of the water, the state of the weather and the type of holding ground. The minimum amounts for each type are given right. When calculating the amount of scope, don't forget to allow for the depth at high water (which can be deduced from the tide tables). Be careful not to pick an anchoring spot where you could foul another boat when the rode is fully extended, or where there may be obstructions on the seabed. The chart of the area should indicate where you may safely anchor.

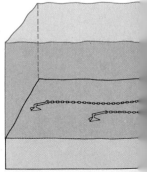

Types of anchor and rode

There are two main categories of anchor: the traditional heavy anchor, such as the fisherman's, which relies mainly on its weight for its holding ability, and the more lightweight modern anchors that rely on their burying ability for holding power. Although the modern type are easier to handle, they may not hold so well in rocky or weedy ground and under these conditions a traditional anchor might do a better job. Your boat, in any event, should have at least two anchors on board – one of them a light anchor of any type, known as a kedge, used for short stops or as a second anchor. The type of rode is important. You can choose between chain or nylon line. Chain is heavy and expensive, but its weight produces a more pronounced curve on the chain in the water and the pull on the anchor is therefore closer to the horizontal than you would get on lighter nylon, thereby reducing the chance of the anchor dragging. Nylon line, however, being stretchy, absorbs shocks well. You can use a mixture of chain and line – say 9m (30ft) of chain from the anchor, and nylon for the remainder.

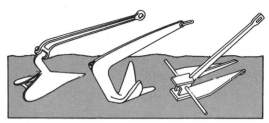

Above, modern lightweight anchors which are capable of holding many times their own weight, particularly in good holding ground. Reading from the left, they are: a CQR, a Bruce and a Danforth anchor. The latter is easy to stow and makes a good kedge anchor.

Right, a traditional fisherman's anchor. If you have enough stowage space, a heavy anchor of this type can be very useful.

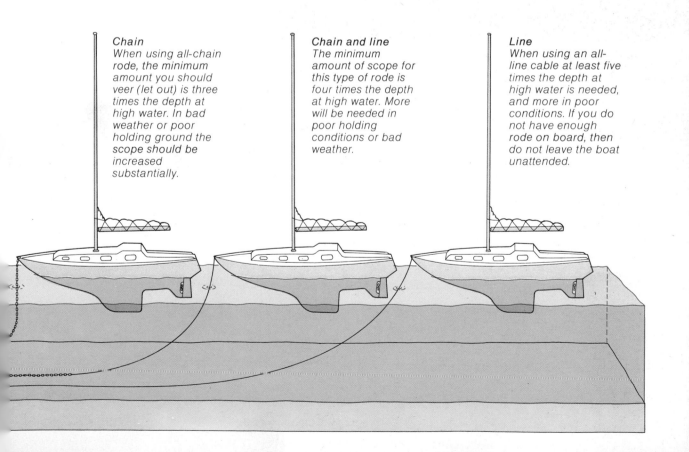

Chain
When using all-chain rode, the minimum amount you should veer (let out) is three times the depth at high water. In bad weather or poor holding ground the scope should be increased substantially.

Chain and line
The minimum amount of scope for this type of rode is four times the depth at high water. More will be needed in poor holding conditions or bad weather.

Line
When using an all-line cable at least five times the depth at high water is needed, and more in poor conditions. If you do not have enough rode on board, then do not leave the boat unattended.

Choosing an anchorage

It is important to choose the site carefully when planning to lie to an anchor, if you want a trouble-free stay. There are several considerations to be taken into account before you can drop the anchor. You must know what the holding ground is like – you can usually get information on the type of seabed from the appropriate chart for the area, or a pilot book, or by using the lead line (see page 74). If the ground is not suitable for whatever anchor you have aboard, you must look for an alternative anchorage. Another point to bear in mind is the length of your anchor rode. The water must be shallow enough for your boat to be able to lie to the correct amount of scope, but it must also be deep enough, in tidal waters, to keep the boat afloat even at low tide. If you anchor at any time other than high tide, then you have to calculate what the depth will be at high water and allow sufficient scope for that depth. Always try to choose an anchorage which is sheltered from the wind as much as possible, and out of a strong tidal stream. If the boat is out of a busy traffic area, you will have a more comfortable stay, because the boat won't roll around in the wash of passing vessels. In a crowded anchorage, you must take particular care that the swinging circle of your boat will not intersect with other boats. With boats of a similar type you can usually allow the swinging circles to intersect a little without danger of collision, as the boats will normally move in the same arc. Boats of different design may be affected quite differently by the tide or the wind. Boats with a lot of windage and not much underwater area will be more affected by wind than tide, but deep-keeled boats with little windage may swing more to the tide, for example. The swinging circles in these circumstances should not intersect. To calculate the swinging circle of other boats near your own, you need to find out where exactly their anchors lie. If there is no one on board to ask, then try to estimate the position from the direction and type of anchor rode, and from the water depth. If in any doubt, stay on board. As the new arrival, it is your responsibility not to foul another boat, and you will have to move if there is any danger of doing so.

Opposite, a sheltered and peaceful anchorage on a river, at sunset.

Choosing a mooring

When choosing a mooring, the considerations of water depth, and shelter from wind and traffic that apply to anchorages must also be taken into account. In addition, you must make sure that the mooring you choose is not a private one, and that it is designed to take the weight of your boat. Many moorings are marked with the maximum size of boat they hold. If you pick up a mooring that is too light for your boat and it breaks while you are there, you will be responsible for the damage caused. When picking up a mooring, it is best if you check immediately with the harbor master that it is both suitable and available for you to use. Swinging room on moorings is not usually a problem, as they are laid with regard to the size of boat that will pick them up. Also the mooring cable has a shorter scope than that of an anchor.

The crew, having checked the mooring is large enough to hold the boat, brings the pick-up buoy on board.

Dropping and weighing anchor

Before dropping anchor, the equipment must be made ready. Remove the anchor from the stowing point, and hang it over the bow fitting, with the rode holding it made fast on a cleat, or around a bollard. Pull the full amount of the rode likely to be needed from the locker and flake it down carefully on the deck, so that it will run free when the anchor is lowered. Make the rode fast. If there is any danger of the anchor being fouled on the bottom, secure a shorter tripping line (equal to the depth of water) to its crown with a buoy on the other end. The tripping line can be used to release the anchor if it does foul. When the boat reaches the anchoring spot, the skipper instructs the crew to let go, using a pre-arranged signal. The crew uncleats the rode holding the anchor in position, and lowers the anchor, letting the rode run out under control until the anchor hits the seabed. The remainder is then veered. If the anchor fails to bite (you can feel a strain on the rode when it does), veer out some additional rode. If it still fails to bite, raise the anchor, check that it isn't fouled with weed, for example, and then try again. To weigh anchor, bring the boat over the anchoring point, either by hauling on the rode or by motoring or sailing into position, while the crew brings in the rode. When its angle is vertical, the boat will be

With the jib ready for hoisting, the crew weighs anchor, one person hauls in the rode, while the other stows it in the locker.

over the anchor and the crew signals this fact to the skipper. The crew then continues to haul on the cable until the anchor is freed, once again signalling to the skipper. The anchor is then brought carefully on board, and cleaned off before stowing. If the anchor doesn't pull free on the rode, use the tripping line.

Laying an anchor from a dinghy

There will be occasions when you will need to lay an anchor from the dinghy, such as when leaving an alongside berth in an onshore wind. You should use a rigid rather than an inflatable dinghy, and a line rather than a chain rode. Tie the dinghy fore and aft alongside the boat, while you organize the equipment. Then tie a light line to the anchor, hang the anchor over the stern of the dinghy, and secure the other end of the line to the thwart, so that you can release the anchor easily while remaining seated. Attach the anchor rode to the anchor and flake it in the stern of the dinghy, starting with the anchor end. When sufficient rode is flaked for the depth, make the other end fast to a strong point on board the cruiser. Row the dinghy to the anchoring point and

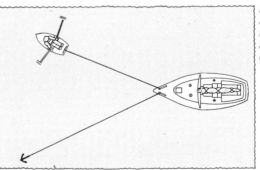

Laying a kedge anchor in addition to the main anchor, using the dinghy.

when all the rode has run out, undo the light line and allow the anchor to drop. Someone on board the boat should take in any slack on the rode until the anchor bites. To retrieve an anchor without moving the cruiser, use the dinghy again, and pull it along the anchor rode until the rode dips vertically. Break the anchor out, ship it and return to the boat, pulling on the rode.

Laying two anchors

There are some situations when you may find it necessary or advisable to lay two anchors. Some boats, multi-hulls and high-sided cruisers in particular, will not lie steadily in certain wind and tide conditions. The solution is to lay a kedge anchor in addition to the main anchor, as shown below right. However, if the wind or tide conditions are likely to change, this method will not work, as the anchor rodes will foul as the boat swings. You would then have to use the method, right, which is normally used for reducing the swinging circle of a boat in a crowded anchorage. In this method, the main anchor is dropped and the boat allowed to drift back on the wind or tide. When twice as much rode as needed has been paid out, the kedge is dropped. The boat is then pulled forward on the main rode and the kedge rode let out until the boat is positioned midway between the two anchors. You then join the rodes at a point far enough down to clear the keel, with either a rolling hitch (for line) or with a shackle (for chain). You should cleat the rodes so that the main rode takes all the strain. Now and again, in exposed conditions or very bad weather, you may want to lay two anchors in tandem to increase the holding power. If you can, use two anchors of the same type, preferably CQR anchors. Shackle an extra 10m (33ft) of chain from the tripping line eye of one anchor to the crown of the other anchor (if the eye is strong enough; if not, shackle the chain around the shank). Use the method for dropping anchor in the usual way.

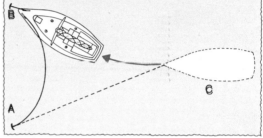

The main anchor (A) and the kedge anchor (B) have been laid, and the rodes joined with a rolling hitch at C to reduce the swinging circle of the boat.

Drop the main anchor (A). Drift back to set it and then motor to B to drop the kedge at an angle of 45° to the line of the first anchor. Drift back to C to adjust the rodes.

Picking up and leaving a mooring

Before the mooring is reached, the crew must be ready with a boat-hook and a line, so that they can pick up the mooring and attach it rapidly as the boat stops with the buoy alongside the bow. The way in which the boat is secured to the mooring depends to some extent on whether you use your own line or the rope strop or chain attached to the buoy. The routine for leaving depends on the method used for securing the boat. If it has been made fast with its own line to a ring on the buoy, then the securing line should be exchanged for a slip line, so that the crew can release it quickly when the skipper gives the order to let go. If the mooring buoy itself has been brought on board, or a rope strop from the mooring, then the rope or chain can be uncleated and held with just a turn around the cleat until the order to let go is given.

One crew member has fetched the mooring pick-up buoy with a boat-hook; the other hauls in.

Arriving and leaving

Boat handling for anchoring and mooring are virtually the same – only the crew routines for handling the equipment will differ. The principle requisite is for the skipper to be able to control boat speed and direction precisely so the crew can drop the anchor, or pick up the mooring, without difficulty. In the case of anchoring, you must make sure that the boat is moving slowly, preferably backwards, when you give the signal to drop anchor. If not, you may find that all the rode falls on top of the anchor, possibly fouling it. Once you have anchored, take several compass bearings or a range (see page 68) to make sure that the anchor is holding firm. When coming up to a mooring, approach with

it on the leeward or downtide bow so that you drift towards it, not away from it.

When leaving an anchorage or a mooring, it is important to plan your route carefully, so that the boat does not interfere with other craft. Always remember to brief the crew properly and give them enough time to get the equipment ready. If you are planning to use the engine, switch it on early enough to give it time to warm up.

Under power

After choosing your anchoring spot or mooring buoy, you must decide how to approach. You should always head the boat into the element which has the greatest effect on it. This will help to slow the boat down once the engine is put in neutral, and will give you greater control. Look at the way other boats similar to your own are lying, to gauge the strongest element. Make sure that the crew are properly briefed and have the equipment ready. In the case of anchoring make sure that the boat has stopped and is starting to move backwards as you drop anchor, and in the case of mooring, aim to stop with the buoy on the bow. When leaving under power, you

must first consider your route away from the anchorage or mooring buoy. Since the boat will point into the strongest element when lying to the anchor or mooring, you should also leave in that direction, unless prevented by an obstruction. If you are anchored, you will have to weigh anchor before motoring off, and if moored, you can simply drop the mooring buoy clear of the boat as you leave.

Under sail

In order to travel in with some control over boat speed, your final approach will be under either mainsail or headsail. The choice of sail depends on whether the wind is forward, on or aft of the beam when the boat is on its final approach and when lying to the anchor or mooring. You therefore have to establish how your boat will lie, and it may be a good idea to sail around the area first to assess the situation. Give the crew plenty of time to get the deck gear ready and lower and stow whichever sail is not being used. Your speed can be controlled by easing the sheets as you approach. If you are approaching a mooring, remember to stop with the boat facing into the strongest element. If the wind is forward of the beam, approach under mainsail alone. Sail in on a close reach and let the sail flap to stop. If you approach with the wind aft of the beam lower the mainsail and come in under headsail alone. Then lower the headsail or allow it to flap, and drift up to the appropriate point.

When leaving the same principles apply. With the

wind forward of the beam leave under mainsail alone but have the headsail hanked on ready for immediate hoisting. When lying to a mooring, you can control your point of departure by using the mooring rope. Pull it back to the windward shroud before releasing it to give the boat more steerage way and to allow it to turn onto the desired course. With the wind aft of the beam, hoist the headsail and immediately drop the mooring, or raise the anchor. Steer into clear water before hoisting the mainsail. When anchored in strong winds, delay hoisting the headsail until the anchor has been broken out.

Opposite, after sailing up to the mooring the crew passes a temporary slip line through the mooring buoy ring while the mainsail is lowered.

DRYING OUT

In some tidal waters you will find that the harbor dries out at low water. Boats with a single keel are inherently less stable than those with bilge keels, or with some form of twin keel, but different keel profiles react in various ways. Try to keep the weight balanced fore and aft as well as laterally. You must, of course, take sensible precautions to ensure that your boat doesn't get damaged during the drying-out process, and that it is properly secured.

If you are tying up in an unfamiliar port, try and find out about the nature of the ground on which the keel of the boat will be resting. Is it strewn with rocks or rubbish, for example? Does the ground slope away sharply from the quay wall? If you cannot get reliable advice, then it would be sensible to take a mooring in deeper water if available, or anchor off, and study the ground at low tide before deciding whether to come in or not on the next tide.

Once you have selected a suitable spot to dry out, your next task is to make sure that the boat stays upright as it dries. In fact it is safest if it leans at a very slight angle towards the wall — no greater than 10° off the vertical. To achieve this very slight slant it helps to shift some ballast onto the appropriate side-deck (your anchor chain, fuel or water containers will probably be adequate for the task). As the tide falls, position your fenders so that the sides of the boat are protected from chafe against the harbor wall. Where possible, you should use a fender board to keep the fenders in place and to protect them. Your bow and stern lines should be fastened a long way fore and aft of the boat so that their angle is not too acute at low water. You will have to adjust them as the tide falls, and again as it rises. Your springs should be fastened in the usual way and adjusted with the ebb and flow of the tide. Check that the springs don't become fouled on the lifelines or fenders, and if you have open fairleads, make sure you lash the lines into them so that they can't slip out as the tide falls.

You need to be careful that your boat doesn't stray away from the wall as the tide drops — if it does, you could damage your lifelines, rigging and mast, if not all three. Weight the bow and stern lines as shown below to help prevent this occurring.

If you are drying out in an unfamiliar port don't leave the boat unattended. Once it has taken the ground comfortably, however, you can safely go ashore.

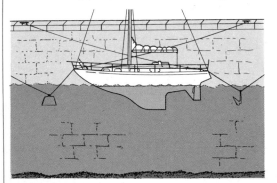

Above, attach an anchor or some other weight to the bow and stern lines to prevent the boat straying away from the wall. The weights will pull the slack down, keeping the lines taut.

Right, drying out against a wall can provide you with the opportunity to carry out general mainten-ance and repairs.

SPINNAKERS

Most Marconi sloops tend to be under-powered on downwind courses in light winds. One solution is to supplement your cruising sail wardrobe with a spinnaker. Although some cruising skippers are wary of spinnakers, regarding them as the province of the committed racing sailor, they can be used without too much difficulty on downwind and broad reaching courses in light to moderate breezes.

Using a spinnaker will involve purchasing and fitting the extra equipment necessary – spinnaker pole, sheets and guys, uphaul and downhaul, a halyard and fittings for the pole on the mast. The crew will have to learn how to handle the sail properly – how to get it up and down without foul-ups, and how to set it properly. Nowadays, however, you can buy a special fitting – a sausage-like sock – which is used to make hoisting and lowering easier. It operates by encasing the sail in the sock until it is hoisted. The sock is then pulled up to the head of the sail allowing the spinnaker to be broken out and set in the usual way. To lower the sail, the procedure is reversed, and has the advantage that no packing is needed, the spinnaker simply being stowed in the sock.

Types of spinnaker

Spinnakers are made of special lightweight rip-resistant nylon sailcloth. The fabric has elasticity and is cut in panels to give predictable stretch properties. To a large extent the way the sail performs is determined by the cut of the panels.
Generally, the fuller cuts are reserved for downwind courses, the flatter cuts used on courses closer to the wind. The two basic cuts, the radial and the horizontal cut, both tend to have the disadvantage that they stretch at the foot and the head respectively. The combination cuts, the tri-radial and radial head, have largely eliminated this problem and produce a good all-purpose spinnaker. The radial head is possibly better suited to light winds. A fifth type, the star-cut spinnaker, is useful for courses close to the wind as it holds a flatter shape under wind pressure. The type you choose will be determined by the sort of sailing you undertake, and the experience of yourself and your crew.

Star-Cut   Tri-radial   Radial head

Radial   Horizontal

Spinnaker cut
Five different cuts of spinnaker are shown above and left. They come in a wide variety of colors, but there is no particular significance in the choice of colors, apart from personal preference. The spinnaker cloth has greater stretch properties on the diagonal than it does with the weave and this factor is taken into account in the construction of the spinnaker.

Spinnaker cloth weave

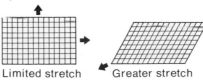

Limited stretch   Greater stretch

Parts of the spinnaker

The spinnaker is a symmetrical triangular sail which is not attached by its luff to a spar, but is set flying from the halyard. The means of controlling the set of the sail is by sheets and guys, led from the clews of the sail to the cockpit, and by a rigid spinnaker pole fixed at one end to the mast and at the other to one clew of the sail. The arrangement, right, is a typical one for a medium-sized cruiser. Smaller boats may have only one sheet and guy, and the uphaul/downhaul may be attached to the center of the pole.

Guys

The guy is the line which is led from the supported clew of the spinnaker to the cockpit. In this system, a guy is rigged on each side of the boat. It is fastened to the clew with a snap shackle and led outside all the rigging to a block just forward of the cockpit, and thence to a winch.

Sheets

The sheet is the line from the unsupported clew of the spinnaker. As with the guys, one is rigged on each side of the boat. They are fastened by a snap shackle to the ring on the guy, rather than the clew of the sail. They are led similarly to the guys, but through a block on each quarter, and are usually of a different color to prevent confusion.

Halyard

You can use a spare headsail halyard for the spinnaker, but it is better to have a separate spinnaker halyard, since the pull on the spinnaker when it is flown covers a larger arc than the pull on the headsail halyard, and it therefore needs to be led through a block that is free to turn through the necessary angle before being led down inside the mast to deck level.

Spinnaker pole

The spinnaker pole is usually made of aluminum and has a piston release system at either end to clip it to the mast and the guy. It is positioned using an uphaul and downhaul, the arrangement of which may vary according to the size and design of the system. A sliding bracket on the mast allows the pole height to be adjusted.

Winches

On most medium-sized cruisers separate winches are fitted for the spinnaker guys and sheets. They are normally positioned just aft of the standard winches used for the genoa, and are often smaller and less powerful. There are times when it is useful to be able to use the genoa sheet winches as well, and you can usually do this since the genoa is normally lowered.

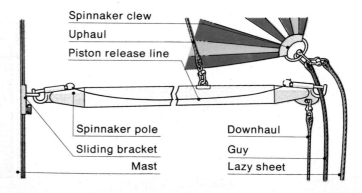

Spinnaker clew
Uphaul
Piston release line
Spinnaker pole
Sliding bracket
Mast
Downhaul
Guy
Lazy sheet

Hoisting a spinnaker

Even a simple headsail can be hoisted incorrectly if it hasn't been properly bagged up. With a spinnaker, which can easily get out of control, it is imperative that it is correctly bagged each time.
To hoist the spinnaker, secure the bag to the pulpit, or to the leeward lifelines, if your headsail system uses hanks. Open the top of the bag and attach the halyard to the head, and a sheet and guy to each clew. (On small boats you may only need to attach a sheet or a guy to each clew). See that the guys and sheets are led outside all the rigging to their blocks on the side-decks, and then to a winch. Before hoisting, steer onto a broad reach. Clip the inboard end of the pole to the mast fitting and attach the uphaul and downhaul. Clip the windward guy to the pole end and raise the pole to the horizontal, using the uphaul. Hoist the sail, pulling quickly on the halyard, having first put a turn on the winch. Cleat the halyard as soon as the sail is fully hoisted. Winch in the guy to pull the sail to the pole end, and to get the pole more or less at right angles to the apparent wind. Cleat it, and then pull in the sheet until the sail fills. Lower the headsail, furl it and tie it to the lifelines.

1 Attach the spinnaker head to the spinnaker halyard.

2 Attach the guys and sheets to the clews (or guy and sheet in a simple system). Lead the lines back to the cockpit, outside the rigging.

3 Clip the inboard end of the pole to the mast.

4 Clip the outer end of the pole to the guy. Check that all lines are correctly rigged. Steer onto a broad reach.

5 Attach the uphaul/downhaul and raise the pole to the horizontal using the uphaul. Hoist the spinnaker quickly and cleat the halyard.

6 Winch in the guy to pull the sail to the pole end, and then cleat·it. Pull in the sheet until the sail fills, far right, and then lower the headsail and furl it.

Trimming the spinnaker

The three main factors that affect the set of the spinnaker are the sheet tension and the height and fore-and-aft position of the spinnaker pole. If you set the clews of the spinnaker at roughly the same height you will achieve a symmetrical set to the sail. You can alter only the height of the clew attached to the pole. This is done by adjusting the pole height using the uphaul and downhaul system, and by the sliding track on the mast, if your boat has one. Try to keep the pole horizontal at all times, as this helps to keep the sail as far out from the boat as possible.

You will find that the sail drops if the wind does, and you will have to lower the pole to keep the two clews level. As the wind increases, the sail will rise and you should adjust the pole height accordingly. Once you are satisfied with the pole height, you can tighten the downhaul to prevent the spinnaker from lifting the pole any higher. On small cruisers the uphaul and downhaul are usually fixed to the middle of the pole, but in larger boats they are often attached to the outboard end. In the latter types of system, the downhaul will lead from the pole end to a point near the bow, and acts as a foreguy as well as a down-haul. You will have to adjust it whenever you alter the pole position with the guy. The angle of the pole fore and aft is adjusted by the guy. In general, the pole should be kept at right angles to the apparent wind, as shown by the burgee.

Once you are satisfied that the pole is correctly positioned you can cleat the guy and simply use the sheet to make any fine adjustments. However, if it is difficult to keep the spinnaker filled, you may need to let the pole forward a little. If you have an expert crew, they can play the sheet continuously to get the best possible set. If not, you may be advised to fill the sail, cleat the sheet and use your own skills as a helmsman to prevent the spinnaker from collapsing. The wind strength and direction will determine the way in which your spinnaker is set and played. In all but light winds you may need to put someone to work at winching in the sheet, while another crew member tails on the sheet and watches the spinnaker. In light winds, and with moderate-sized cruising spinnakers, the winch handle won't be necessary. Although most spinnakers can be carried when the wind is slightly forward of the beam, the majority of cruiser skippers will find it better to drop the spinnaker on beam reaches and change to a large genoa.

Right, the spinnaker sheet trimmer has succeeded in getting the sail to set perfectly by keeping the luff on the point of curling.

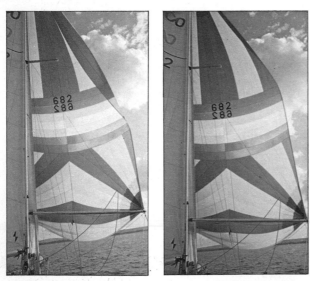

To get a perfect set to the spinnaker, ease the sheet until the luff begins to curl (above, left) and then slowly pull it in until the curl disappears (above, right). To succeed you must keep the clews level, adjusting the pole height if necessary (right).

Dip-pole jibe

This method is the most commonly used in medium-to large-sized cruising boats, as it allows you to keep reasonable control of the spinnaker. However, you should use it only if two guys and two sheets are rigged. With a single guy and sheet you should use the end-for-end jibe, below.

To carry out a dip pole jibe, the helmsman steers onto a run. The spinnaker is trimmed for this point of sailing and the sheet and guy are cleated. A crew member goes forward, taking a loose bight of the lazy guy with him. Using the piston release line at the mast end of the pole, he detaches the pole from the working guy and moves forward to the pulpit. Another crew member in the cockpit, or the helmsman (if short-handed), eases out the uphaul and pulls in the downhaul so that the pole end dips down, and it can be swung forward to the bow of the boat. (The forward crew member may have had to raise the pole on the mast to allow the outboard end of the pole to clear the headstay.) If an inner headstay is rigged it will have to be unclipped if possible, failing that, an end-for-end jibe must be used. The forward crew member guides the pole past the headstay to the new side and clips the new working guy onto the pole end. The cockpit crew hauls on the uphaul to raise the pole and winches on the new working guy to move the pole aft, into its correct setting position. The helmsman should jibe the mainsail once the spinnaker has been jibed; once he has done so, the spinnaker guy and the new working sheet are used to trim the sail for the new course. The old guy and sheet, now the lazy guy and sheet, are left slack.

The pole is tripped from the guy and lowered to the foredeck.

The pole, with the new guy clipped on, is passed inside the headstay.

The mainsail is jibed and the pole raised to the spinnaker clew.

The pole angle is adjusted to suit the new course by trimming the guy.

End-for-end jibe

If your boat has a simple spinnaker system with only one sheet and guy, and with the uphaul/downhaul fitted into the center of the spinnaker pole, you should use an end-for-end jibe. The helmsman puts the boat onto a run, the sail is trimmed and the sheet and guy cleated. A crew member then releases the pole from the guy using the piston release line, and detaches the pole from the mast. The inboard end of the pole is then moved across the boat, and attached to the new guy (formerly the working sheet). The pole is pushed out on the new side and re-attached to the mast.

Meanwhile the helmsman jibes the mainsail. The spinnaker is trimmed to suit the new course.

Beware of attempting this type of jibe in anything greater than light or moderate winds. Because the sail is not fixed to the pole for part of the operation, you run the risk that it may get out of control. You will either have to lower the spinnaker, jibe and hoist it again, or change the spinnaker for a poled-out genoa.

Right, even racing crews make mistakes: this tangle, known as an hourglass, was caused by incorrect handling during a jibe. The crew must react fast to sort out the problem before it gets worse.

Lowering the spinnaker

Before lowering the spinnaker you should hoist and trim the headsail, so that the spinnaker cannot wrap itself around the forestay, if mishandled. The skipper should steer the boat onto a broad reach and then the corner of the sail at the pole end should be released to empty the sail of wind. In small boats you may find it is enough to allow the guy to run, but in larger boats a crew member will have to go forward and trip the snap shackle that holds the guy to the clew of the sail. As a result, the spinnaker will fly out like a flag in the lee of the mainsail. A crew member in the hatchway should hold onto a bight of the lazy guy, or the sheet itself, with a small spinnaker. As soon as the crew member up forward has tripped the tack he can begin to pull in on the line to bring the spinnaker clew under the boom and into the hatchway. As he hauls in, another crew member should ease out the halyard and the sail should be bundled down into the hatchway. Don't let the halyard out too quickly or the spinnaker will end up in the water. Once the sail is down, the pole is stowed and the sheets, guys and halyards are disconnected from it and stowed. The sail is then packed carefully into its bag (bottom).

  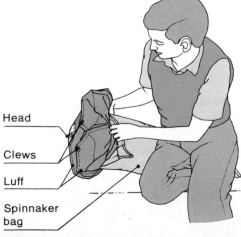

1 Prior to lowering the spinnaker, the headsail is hoisted and trimmed.

2 The spinnaker guy is tripped from the pole end to allow the sail to flap in the lee of the mainsail.

3 Using the lazy guy (or the sheet on simple systems) the sail is pulled in under the main boom, bundled down the hatchway and carefully packed below-decks.

Packing the spinnaker

To make sure that the spinnaker is free of twists when it is hoisted, it must be packed properly below-decks after lowering. It is easiest if one person takes the responsibility for packing the sail and works in the following manner: he finds the head of the sail, and puts it to one side while he works down each luff in turn until he finds both clews. He then keeps the head, clews and luffs to one side, untwisted, while he packs the center part of the sail in to the spinnaker bag. The last parts to enter the bag are therefore the luffs, head and clews. He allows these to protrude from the bag and ties a short length of line to them so that they are immediately identifiable and accessible the next time that the sail is used. Packed in this way, the spinnaker should be free of twists when hoisted.

Head
Clews
Luff
Spinnaker bag

Tri-radial spinnakers, right, flown and set perfectly on a beam reach. Headsails are being used by these racing boats to provide extra drive.

REDUCING SAIL

As the wind strength increases, there will come a point when a boat can no longer carry full canvas if it is to perform both comfortably and efficiently. The point will vary according to the design and size of the boat, and although, in general, large boats will be able to carry full sail in stronger winds than small boats can, much depends on other factors, such as the state of the sea, the size of the working sails and the underwater profile of the boat, for example.

There are two basic ways of reducing the sail area: you can exchange the sail for a smaller one or you can reduce its size by reefing it in any one of a number of ways. In practice the two are often combined; for example, you may exchange the existing headsail for a smaller one and then reduce the area of the mainsail by reefing it. In general, the mainsail is too large and bulky for it to be swopped for a smaller sail, although, in very strong winds, when you may not be able to reduce the mainsail enough, you could substitute a trysail for it. Recent developments in headsail reefing gear now allow you to reef the headsail efficiently, instead of changing down to a smaller sail. This has two advantages: you need not carry so many sails on board, and the likelihood of the crew having to work on the foredeck in bad weather is greatly reduced.

There are no fixed rules about when to reef: each skipper should be aware of the limitations of his own boat and should be able to feel when the boat is overpressed: the obvious signs are when the leeward rail is awash or if the helmsman is having difficulty holding the boat on course. Once you feel the need to reef, you should waste no time in doing so, unless you are about to enter harbor, or if a reduction in wind strength is expected very shortly.

It is important to keep the sails balanced so that the boat continues to sail well, and you should therefore be careful to reef the headsail and mainsail in proportion to prevent excessive lee or weather helm developing. Normally, you would reduce the size of the headsail first – by changing down to a smaller sail or by taking in a reef – and your next step would be to reef the mainsail. If the wind strength continued to increase or if the boat was still overpressed, you would continue to make further reductions in both headsail and mainsail size as necessary.

When taking in a reef or changing headsails, you should slow the boat down so that the crew are not thrown off-balance or soaked by waves when working on the foredeck. If you put the boat on a broad reach the mainsail will partially blanket the headsail from the wind, and any pitching at the bow will be reduced to a minimum. The crew should be told to wear their harnesses and clip on their lifelines so that they have both hands free to work. If you reef the mainsail, do it with the boat hove-to or on a close reach, so that the sail does not fill with wind. To avoid any accidents, tell the crew never to stand to leeward of a flogging sail, or on a headsail lying on the deck – it is usually both wet and slippery.

Below, a cruiser-racer being reefed using a jiffy reefing system. The lines from the leech of the sail are the reefing pendants.

Mainsail jiffy reefing

Jiffy reefing is the modern equivalent of points reefing, the traditional method for reducing a sail, in which the sail is lowered a little and the lower part of the sail is lashed to the boom. In a jiffy reefing system, there are reef cringles, in the leech and luff and across the sail, usually at three different heights. The sail can be reefed quickly to the desired size by fitting the luff cringle onto a ram's horn fitting at the gooseneck, and by pulling down the leech by a similar amount using a reefing line, or pendant attached to the leech cringle. Jiffy reefing was first introduced by the offshore yacht racing fraternity who were looking for a quicker way of reefing than the traditional laborious points system. In many ways, this system is more efficient than roller reefing (see overleaf), since it can be carried out by one person who does not even have to move from the cockpit, if a purchase system replaces the ram's horn fitting at the luff. Jiffy reefing gives a better sail shape than does roller reefing, and the equipment needed for it is minimal and, therefore, cheap to fit. To take in a reef you should ease the boom vang and mainsheet and tension the topping lift. If luff slides are fitted to the mainsail, you should remove the mast gate or locking pin. Then lower the halyard until the appropriate luff cringle can be attached to the ram's horn, retension the halyard, and replace the pin. Then pull in the appropriate reefing pendant until the leech cringle is down onto the boom, and cleat the pendant. Release the topping lift, and retension the boom vang. You can then either leave the bunt of the sail lying next to the boom or you can roll it into a sausage shape, and lash it neatly in place. To shake out a reef, you simply reverse the procedure.

Right, the cruiser-racer (opposite) with the reef taken in. Jiffy reefing gives a good reefed sail shape and is quick and easy to carry out.

1 *Having tightened the topping lift and eased the boom vang, lower the mainsail until the luff cringle can be slipped onto the ram's horn fitting. Then retension the halyard.*

2 *Pull in the appropriate reefing pendant until the leech cringle is level with the boom, and stretched aft along it.*

3 *Ease the topping lift and retension the boom vang.*

4 *If you wish, roll up the bunt of the sail into a sausage shape and lash it to the boom with a lacing line.*

Mainsail roller reefing

With the conventional roller reefing system, the mainsail is rolled around the boom, rather like a roller blind, so that the area of the sail can be reduced by the required amount. The boom is rotated using a handle, which is fitted either on the side of the boom near the mast, or on the front of the mast itself. Before you reef a sail using this system, you should tension the topping lift to take the weight of the boom. If the sail has slides at the luff, you should remove the retaining pin or mast gate, and you should also detach the boom vang if it is fitted directly onto the boom. Then ease the mainsail halyard and the mainsheet before rotating the boom. You will find it easier if you have one person to wind in the sail and ease the halyard, and another to pull the leech of the sail aft along the boom, as it is rotated, to prevent the sail bagging in the center and forming a poor shape when reefed. If the battens cannot be rolled in parallel to the boom as it is rotated, they should be removed. Once you have reefed the sail to the required amount, lock the reefing handle in position, retension the halyard and ease the topping lift. Although it is comparatively easy to roller reef a sail in harbor, it is more difficult at sea when it may not be possible to pull the leech out along the boom. As a result the sail doesn't set well. It can also be difficult to get the sail luff wound neatly onto the boom if slides are attached. You will need a special claw attachment for the boom vang so that it can be fitted over the rolled sail. To shake out a reef, simply reverse the method above.

A more recent sophisticated version of roller reefing has been developed, known as in-mast roller reefing. It uses a specially constructed sail, mast and fittings, to overcome the problems of poor sail shape, but it is quite expensive and complex to fit, and as a result has not so far been widely used, except on large boats. It may well, however, become more popular with cruising sailors in the future.

Setting a trysail

In very strong wind conditions it may not be possible to reef the mainsail sufficiently, and a smaller, more specialized sail, known as a trysail, will be needed instead, usually in conjunction with the storm jib. Although the trysail may not be needed very often, it has no real substitute, and any family cruising boat, therefore, would be well advised to carry one, particularly if venturing offshore. You should already have practiced rigging it in reasonably calm conditions so that you know exactly what to do if you need it in bad weather.

The trysail is set without a boom. Lower the mainsail and then the boom, and lash both of them securely on deck. Hoist the trysail in the mast groove as you would for the mainsail. It should, however, be fitted with slides, rather than fed directly into the mast groove. The mast gate or locking pin should be secured and a downhaul tackle led from the tack of the trysail to the base of the mast. The head of the sail should then be shackled to the mainsail halyard, and sheets attached to the clew, either rigged singly or as a two-to-one purchase. The sheets should be led through stout blocks on each quarter of the boat, and then led forward to cockpit winches on the side-decks. Once the sheets have been fastened to the clew and led through the blocks, the sail can be hoisted in the normal way. The height to which it is hoisted is important if the sheets are to be at the appropriate angle to control the sail effectively. It is a good idea to mark the point on the halyard to which the sail should be hoisted during your practice sessions: normally the head of the sail should be at about spreader height. Because the sail is cut at a rising angle from the clew to the tack, the latter will be some way up the mast. The sail shape has been specially designed so that it remains efficient in strong winds, and so that it can be set high enough to clear any waves breaking aboard. Once the sail is hoisted, and the halyard cleated, you can tension the tack downhaul to get a good set to the luff of the sail. If the downhaul is not sufficiently powerful, you could lead it to a winch and then use the winch to tension it. Alternatively, you could use the mainsail halyard to tension the luff. Once you have hoisted the sail, sheet it in on the leeward side, as you would a headsail. Take care not to let the sail flog at any time, since considerable strain will be put on both it and its fittings in strong winds. When tacking or jibing the boat with a trysail set, you should handle the sheets as you would jib sheets. To prevent the sail flogging unnecessarily, take up the slack on the new sheet before easing the old one.

Trysails, like the one opposite, are best colored orange, making them conspicuous in heavy weather.

Headsail furling

Although you would normally change to a smaller headsail as the wind increases in strength, the use of furling or reefing gear can considerably reduce the number of times you have to change down, and the number of sails you need to carry on board. Headsail furling gear is normally only practical if the boat has a headfoil, rather than an ordinary headstay. With furling equipment fitted, you can probably make do with three headsails only: for example, a heavy No. 1 Genoa, a No. 3 Genoa and a storm jib. Since it is not particularly easy to lower a headsail in heavy weather, you would be advised to fit a removable stay behind the foil, so that you can hoist a smaller sail as well, leaving the existing one furled and hoisted. Alternatively, you can set the smaller sail flying.

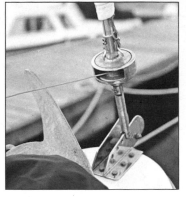

Above, a drum mechanism at the base of the headfoil is used to wind the sail around the stay. Right, a fully furled headsail on its headfoil. The sail should be covered if left rigged, as the fabric may rot if exposed to sunlight for long periods

Headsail reefing

The traditional method for reefing a mainsail is by means of reef points, and some boats incorporate the same system for their headsails. Normally the sail will have one or two rows of cringles, running across the sail, parallel to the foot. If you wish to reef a headsail while it is in use, you must remove and re-attach the sheets. First, remove the lazy sheet and attach it to the appropriate reefing cringle. Then, when you are taking the strain on that sheet to windward, you can remove the other sheet. You can either partly reef the sail by taking in a tri-angular section of the foot, or you can fully reef it by pulling down the luff as well. If you wish to take in a full reef, a reefing line should be rigged through the luff cringle and the tack, and back to a winch and cleat. You then allow the sail to flap slightly while you ease the halyard a little to allow the cringle to be pulled down to the bow fitting. Cleat the reefing line and then retension the luff by pulling on the halyard. Secure the loose fold of the sail, either by passing a lacing cord through the reef cringles or by fastening the reef points.

Above, leading the reefing line from the bow fitting, through the cringle and the tack, to a cleat. Above right, with the halyard eased, the reefing line is pulled to bring the cringle down to the bow fitting. Right, the reefing line is cleated and the bunt of the sail secured with cord or reef points.

ROUGH WEATHER TECHNIQUES

Strong winds and large waves, although alarming for an inexperienced crew, rarely pose a real danger to either the boat, provided that it is seaworthy, or the people aboard, if the skipper, navigator and crew know how to deal with the situation. It is important to make sure that the equipment is strong and well-secured, so that it is able to cope with the extra loads imposed by strong winds and large seas. Small boats can usually cope surprisingly well with buffeting in rough weather, although the skipper may find that the crew does not react quite as well: an inexperienced crew, in particular, is likely to get weak and tired in conditions where a more experienced one is enjoying an exciting sail. Certain points of sailing impose more of a strain than others on both boat and crew, such as beating to windward for any length of time.

The skipper must take proper safety precautions in large waves and strong winds. He and his crew should wear safety harnesses and clip them on before leaving the companionway. Everyone on deck should be warmly dressed, with proper waterproof clothing; hot drinks and energy-giving food should be provided at frequent intervals. Watches should be reduced to the minimum length of time feasible, so that nobody becomes overtired.

If the skipper is caught out in rapidly worsening weather, he must decide what course of action to take: whether to head for port or attempt to ride out the storm at sea. He must do everything within his power to reduce the strain on the boat, changing down to storm sails or, if necessary, running under bare poles.

The forces involved when sailing in heavy weather are tremendous and the boat, and all its equipment, must be capable of withstanding the loads imposed.

Wind and sea state

What exactly constitutes rough weather? Normally a Force 7 (28–33 knots) is regarded as a yachtsman's gale, but for most cruising families rough weather starts slightly earlier – even at a Force 5 (17–21 knots), right, if the boat is beating to windward. The weather forecasts will normally provide frequent and usually accurate warnings of bad weather to come, and the skipper with an inexperienced crew should modify his passage plan accordingly. In a Force 7 (28–33 knots) with the sea state as shown right, the skipper of an average family cruising boat should have changed down to small sails and have stowed all loose equipment. He would then normally head for a safe port.

In a Force 8 (34–40 knots), for example, conditions at sea in a small yacht would be most uncomfortable, and should be avoided if possible. The sails carried would be a storm jib and deep-reefed mainsail or trysail, at the most, and unless the nearest port is to windward and easy to enter, steps should be taken to get enough sea-room to heave-to or lie a-hull until the weather moderates.

Force 5 (17–21 knots): fresh breeze
The waves will be moderate with frequent white caps and some spray. Average wave height will be about 1.8m (6ft). Family crews may get tired beating to windward in these conditions.

Force 7 (28–33 knots): near gale
The seas begin to pile up with waves reaching an average of 4m (13ft 6in). Often known as a yachtsman's gale, the conditions are usually bad enough to encourage most family cruising boats to take shelter if possible.

Preparation and tactics

If bad weather is threatened, the skipper has to decide whether to head for port or to try and ride out the weather at sea. If a sheltered port with a known safe entry, and docking or anchoring facilities, is near to hand, then it would be sensible to head for it, provided there is no danger of meeting shallow water, a lee shore, or hostile conditions on the way. You should always try to make for shelter to windward if possible – if the harbor is on a lee shore, for example, you would be advised to stay out at sea. Once in harbor, double up all the lines and do not attempt to leave until the bad weather has passed over. If you have to ride out the storm at sea, you should head for open water, with as much searoom to leeward as possible, so that there is no danger of your drifting onto the shore (bearing in mind any likely change in wind direction).

Your next task is to prepare the boat for the weather ahead. All loose equipment and items such as the dinghy and life raft should be securely double-lashed down. Equipment below-decks must also be securely stowed away so that it will not fall out of lockers when the boat heels. Check that the hatches are secured and that ventilators, if likely to leak, are plugged. Fasten the companionway washboards and open them only for access, when required. Get the crew to dress in warm clothing, and to put on their safety harnesses. Lifelines must be clipped on as each crew member emerges from the companionway – an unexpected lurch of the boat could easily send someone overboard, if unprepared, and not clipped on, as they tried to climb out of the companionway into the cockpit. As soon as you realize that bad weather is approaching, ask a crew member to go below and prepare flasks of hot soup and some sandwiches or even a hot meal, if there is time to eat it before the rough conditions build up. Get the crew to take anti-seasick tablets, if necessary, Finally pump the bilges out before the rough weather arrives, and at regular intervals once it does. If the visibility is poor, switch on the navigation lights and hoist the radar reflector.

Above, sailing fast and well offwind in fairly hard conditions, this cruiser has a reefed mainsail and medium-sized headsail. If the boat were sailing upwind, the sails would have to be reefed down further.

Left, the skipper of this boat is being unkind to the crew member trying to change the headsail: the boat is sailing quite fast to windward and is pitching into the seas, making the crew's job very difficult — he is bound to get soaked. It would be better to slow the boat down or run before the wind until the sail change is completed.

Sailing in waves

As the wind increases you will have to reduce the sail area by degrees, by reefing the existing sails or exchanging them for smaller ones. If you are beating to windward, you will notice the deterioration in the weather more quickly, and may well have to reduce the sail area quickly. Sailing offwind is more comfortable and should be chosen as a course, where possible. Sailing downwind there is a danger that the boat may travel too quickly and you should use the techniques for slowing the boat, below. If the wind really gets up you may well have to sail under headsail alone or under bare poles. On all points of sailing you should try and approach the waves so that you cause the boat and the crew as little discomfort as possible.

When sailing close-hauled (and only if you must), luff up to meet the crest of the wave and bear away down the back. On reaching courses the boat will be travelling parallel with the waves, and you should try to bear away down the face of particularly large waves at a slight angle to prevent the boat being knocked sideways by them. When running, in fairly strong winds, the boom preventer should be rigged to avoid an accidental jibe. You must make sure that you are not travelling so fast that the boat starts to overtake the wave in front and buries its bow into the back of it. You should reduce sail, or lower it altogether if necessary, and run under bare poles (below).

Lying a-hull

If you wish to pause for a rest, to repair equipment, or to ride out a gale you can either heave-to (see page 73 or lie a-hull. Heaving-to is a solution in moderately strong winds, only if you have a very small storm jib and trysail, otherwise the strain on the sails and rigging may be too great. If you have not, or if the wind is too strong, and you have sufficient room to leeward to allow you to drift, you should lie a-hull. All the sails should be taken down and the tiller lashed to leeward. In very large seas, the boat may not lie comfortably using this method, and in these circumstances you may have to run before the wind under bare poles, provided you have sufficient searoom downwind.

Under bare poles

When running under bare poles, the boat will make surprising speed. It must be steered constantly downwind, with the helmsman carefully keeping the boat stern-on to the waves, making sure that the boat never wanders off course. If it is travelling too fast and overtaking the waves ahead, or causing the approaching waves to break, the helmsman must try to slow the boat down using either or both of the methods below. In fact, the vast majority of cruising boats can withstand tremendous battering by wind and sea, but the crew, particularly if inexperienced, may become exhausted and incapable long before the boat is in danger.

Slowing the boat

There are various ways of slowing the boat down but the most common is to trail a heavy line – at least 45m (150ft) long – behind the boat. It is most effective if trailed in a loop, or bight, with each end of the line led through a stern fairlead, and around a winch before being cleated. If you don't have a warp long enough, trail two shorter ones, as shown right. Another technique is to trail a drogue, or sea-anchor (an open-ended conical canvas bag) or an improvised one made of a bundle of fenders, or a bucket. However, you may find the drogue, if too long, performs so effectively that it prevents the boat giving way to large waves, which may be dangerous.

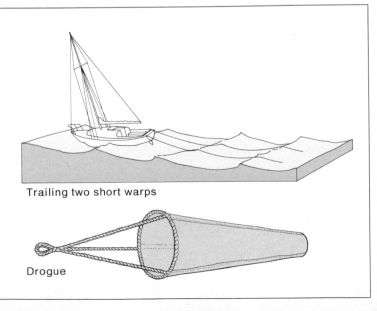

Trailing two short warps

Drogue

MAN OVERBOARD

Losing a man overboard is one of the worst things that can happen at sea, and it is, therefore, vital to make sure that all the crew members, as well as the skipper, know how to tackle the routine for dealing with the situation. After all, it may well be the skipper who goes overboard! The man overboard drill must be practiced regularly, under both sail and power, using a dan buoy and drogue (opposite) as a substitute person. If you are skippering an unfamiliar boat, or have an inexperienced crew on board, you should practice the man overboard drill as one of your first priorities. The drill described overleaf is suitable for all boats under sail, and is quite straightforward to learn.

Although normally you are most likely to be under sail when such an incident occurs, you may well be under power. If you are, the immediate priority is to make sure that the man overboard doesn't get caught in the propeller. If the helmsman sees the person go overboard, he should steer at once towards the side over which the person fell, which will move the stern of the boat (and the blades of the propeller) away from him. The same crew procedures for recovery under sail (overleaf) are carried out, but the course steered differs. You should turn the boat in a tight circle to return to the person in the water, and stop head-to-wind, with the person forward of the cockpit. Once you have secured him to the boat with a lifeline under his armpits, switch off the engine, and get him out of the water as quickly as possible using one of the techniques described overleaf.

If you are sailing when the person goes overboard and your crew are not competent to handle the recovery drill, you may find it advisable to lower the sails and carry out the procedure under power.

If, for any reason, you lose sight of the person in the water, his safe recovery depends on the ability of the helmsman to sail an accurate course. If the exact time when he was lost, and the course sailed are noted, the navigator should be able to calculate the direction of the reciprocal course and the length of time to sail it to bring the boat back to the right place. If you cannot see or hear the person in the water when you do reach the position, you will have to start a square search, below. This depends on accurate control of speed and direction, and is often best done under power. The aim is to cover the area systematically so that you pass within a set distance of the man overboard. The navigator has to plan the course, as shown below, to calculate the legs in terms of distance travelled, at a given speed, for a set time. The length of the legs will depend on the conditions. In average daylight conditions, you should plan to be farther than 50m (165ft) from the estimated position of the man in the water. At night or in fog the distance should be less.

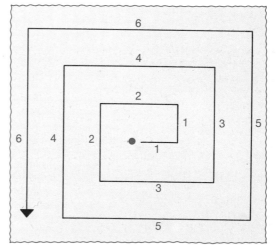

A square search may be needed if the person is lost at night or in fog. The navigator has to calculate the length of the first leg to be twice the maximum distance you want to be from the person. The following legs are increased as shown on the diagram.

Recovery under sail

Whenever a person falls overboard there are several things which must be done very quickly. Someone must throw a lifering and the dan buoy overboard. He should aim the ring upwind of the person in the water so that it has a greater chance of blowing towards him. He must alert the rest of the crew with a cry of "Man overboard" and throw in a second lifering (if there is more than one left) and a dye marker or any floating objects, such as torn up paper, which will mark the position. One crew member must immediately be detailed to watch the man overboard to minimize the risk of losing sight of him. Even a momentary distraction could result in his being lost from view among the waves. While the crew is carrying out these tasks, the person on the helm must immediately start to steer the course shown at right. If the spinnaker is set, it must be quickly lowered. The navigator or helmsman must note the time and course steered — if the person is lost from sight, it may be necessary to use this information to return to the spot. A crew member must prepare two lines to throw to the person in the water when the boat returns. A boat-hook should also be available. Once there is sufficient searoom, the helmsman should tack. (If sailing under the headsail alone, the boat's handling characteristics may dictate that you jibe instead.) It is particularly important that the person watching the man overboard should not take his eyes off him during the turn, as everyone else is likely to become disorientated. Once the boat has turned, the navigator must note the time and new course. The helmsman should aim to stop the boat to windward of the man in the water so that he is alongside the cockpit area, near enough to be reached.

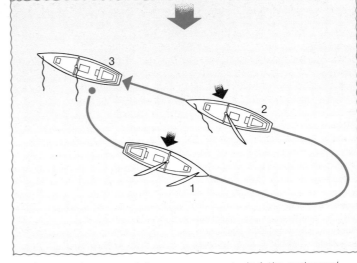

Steer onto a beam reach to the apparent wind (1). When you have enough searoom (about ten boat-lengths), tack onto a close reach to the apparent wind, the reciprocal course (2). Let the headsail fly to slow down and stop the boat to windward of the man overboard (3).

Right, in a man overboard drill the boat has been slowed down sufficiently, and the lifering — the substitute for the person in the water — is about to be picked up.

Getting the person on board

Getting back to someone who has gone overboard is only the first stage of the problem. The second stage, getting him on board, is just as difficult, if not more so. If the person has been in the water for any length of time he will be exhausted and unable to help himself, particularly if the water is cold and he is encumbered by heavy sailing clothes. There are a number of ways you can try to bring him on board, but there are no hard-and-fast rules, and much will depend on the type of boat, the number of crew members able to help, the equipment and the weather. (You would be well advised to try a practice recovery with a willing crew member acting as a guinea pig – he must, of course, be tied to the boat with a lifeline before he goes over the side.) Having reached the man in the water, you must try to grab hold of him, and tie him to the side of the boat by passing a line under his armpits, keeping his head out of the water. Bring him to the cockpit area where it is safe for the crew to work. If the headsail is hoisted, lower it, but keep the mainsail hoisted in all but the worst conditions or if the method of recovery requires the mainsail to be lowered. Get any crew members on deck to wear harnesses and clip themselves on, and then cut the lifelines, if necessary, to make the task of bringing him on board easier. Unfasten the leeward lifelines in the cockpit area so that they don't interfere with the recovery. If you have enough strong crew members aboard,

and the person in the water is conscious and able to help himself, and if the boat has a low freeboard, you can try to lift him out of the water. Face him away from the side of the boat, and grasp him under his armpits. If you have a boarding ladder, you could use that instead, or you could lower a line, with a bowline tied in the end, to give the person a foot-hold. However, you would normally need some form of extra power, in the shape of a purchase system, to get someone on board. You can rig a spare tackle on the end of the boom, or unshackle the boom vang from the mast, and attach it to the end of the boom. The lower end of the purchase can then be fastened to another line tied to the person's armpits, and he can then be hoisted up, and swung aboard. Alternatively, if you have an inflatable dinghy to hand you can launch it, secure it to the boat, and roll the person into it, before hoisting him aboard. Otherwise, use either the mainsail or headsail. With the mainsail, lower it and lash the boom end in the cockpit, and then drop a bight of the mainsail over the leeward side. Float the person into it, and scoop him aboard by hauling on the halyard. With the headsail, you use the same system but lash the foot of the sail to the rail before scooping him aboard in the same manner. Once you have the person on board, treat him for shock and exposure and get medical help if necessary.

A lifeline, tied under the person's armpits and led to a convenient winch, may be enough to haul the person aboard.

A boarding ladder is useful, if the person can help himself, although a lifeline should be tied around him before he tries to clamber aboard.

FOG

The experienced sailor fears fog far more than very bad weather. It presents a greater danger since reduced visibility increases the possibility of collision with another vessel. Always listen to the forecasts before you set out: if fog is expected, stay in harbor until it clears – you would be courting danger by setting out in such conditions.

If you are already at sea when fog descends there is a procedure to minimize the risks. Much will depend on the skill of your navigator, who has to do everything in his power to verify his position, and then to plot a course which takes the boat out of the shipping channel and dangerous or crowded waters. His aim is to keep the boat safe, even at the expense of a prior passage plan.

Your opportunities for detecting other people's presence and advertising your own are through appropriate fog signals, laid down in the International Regulations for Preventing Collisions at Sea, and radar reflectors.

Sound signals

If you are caught in fog, it is your job to make sure people know you are there by sounding the appropriate signals. You are also going to have to identify the sounds made by other vessels. Fog-horns, bells and gongs are all used, and different combinations of these sounds indicate boats making way (travelling under sail or power), or under way (not at anchor or moored but not moving with no way on). or at anchor, or aground. The pattern of sounds also gives a broad indication of the size of the boat concerned. Boats under 12m (39ft) need only carry an "efficient sound signal" usually an aerosol fog-horn, (below). The canisters run out quite rapidly, so always carry spares. If you have to, you can improvise the sounds – beating on a saucepan with a spoon, for

example. Larger boats also carry a bell, and boats over 100m (328ft) make gong signals in addition to the others. Fog-horn signals are short (one second) or long (four to six seconds). Bells are rung as a single ring, or rapid ringing for five seconds. Gongs are always sounded singly. There are rules for the duration and frequency of the sounds to indicate your type of vessel and position. You should keep a reference book on board to remind you of unusual ones – the more common ones are shown below. If you are in a crowded channel, the navigation buoys will also be equipped with sound signals. These will be marked on the appropriate navigation chart for the area, and your navigator must be able to identify them.

Aerosol fog-horn
These days most boats carry an aerosol fog horn. The canisters are renewable, and are screwed into the horn. Depress the button to sound the horn.

Key

▬▬▬ ▪ Fog-horn

▲ Bell

◣◥◣◥ Rapid bell ringing

○ Gong

Under sail
One long blast and two short ones every two minutes (also applies to a boat with restricted maneuverability)

Making way under power
One long blast on the horn every two minutes

Under way
Two long horn blasts at two minute intervals

Aground – under 100m (328ft)
Three bells followed by rapid ringing and another three bells at one-minute intervals

Aground – over 100m (328ft)
Three bells, followed by rapid ringing, three bells and a gong sounded aft every minute

At anchor – under 100m (328ft)
Rapid ringing of the bell forwards at one minute intervals

At anchor – over 100m (328ft)
Rapid ringing of a bell forwards, followed by a gong sounded aft at one minute intervals

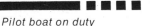

Pilot boat on duty
Normal signals for a boat under power, followed by four short horn blasts every two minutes

Preparation

As soon as fog descends, the skipper and crew should hoist the radar reflector (if not kept permanently hoisted), switch on the navigation lights and begin to make the appropriate fog signals. Crew members should be stationed fore and aft as look-outs to watch and listen for other boats. The crew should don lifejackets, but harness lines should not be clipped on in case there is a collision, and they need to jump clear. Any crew member resting below decks should remain fully clothed, wearing a lifejacket. Noone should remain in the forepeak because of the risk of collision. If possible, the dinghy should be towed behind the boat in case it is needed in a hurry. The liferaft should be at hand, as should red and white flares (see pages 144–45).

It helps to have a rough idea of the visibility. Toss a bundle of paper overboard, and note the length of time it takes to disappear from view. The navigator should then be able to work out the visibility by an equation in which the boat's speed in knots is multiplied by the time in minutes it took for the paper to disappear,

divided by 60, which guides the distance at which another boat will first be seen.

In deep water, keep the boat moving slowly, so that you have enough steerage way to maneuver but are not travelling so fast that you have no time to react if you suddenly come across another boat. In light winds, you may have to use the engine, but it should be switched off from time to time to enable you to listen for other boats. If you have to cross the main shipping channel, do so at right angles and with all possible speed. One way of avoiding possible collision is to head for shallow water which larger vessels cannot negotiate. Other small boats may well have the same idea, so watch out for them. If you do reach shallow, sheltered water, a good procedure is to anchor and to make appropriate signals while keeping a good look out.

Although you will be signalling yourself, and listening for other boats, don't rely on sound signals; keep a careful watch at all times. Look-outs in large ships may be deafened by the noise of their own engines and signals, and may be

unaware of your presence, so never stand on your rights and depend on the other vessel to take avoiding action. If you see another boat, get out of the way.

The first glimpse you may have of another vessel could well be the white bow wave. If it is heading straight towards you, try to turn your boat so that is no longer at right angles to the approaching vessel – preferably try to get your own boat end-on to the approaching one. It will give you the greatest chance of being pushed aside by the bow wave and thus avoiding a collision. Similarly, if you find your boat is on a converging course with another, turn to face in the same direction so that the force of the blow will be minimized.

Radar reflectors

Large commercial vessels always carry radar equipment which is switched on in poor visibility. If your sailing boat is to stand any chance of being picked up on the radar screen of a larger vessel, you must have a radar reflector of a suitable size, mounted where it can operate effectively. If should be no smaller in diameter than 60cm (2ft) and preferably larger. Since the reflector works by returning the radar waves emitted from the larger vessel's radar equipment, it should always be mounted where it can easily reflect the signals. The sails (or any other item) of the boat's equipment) must not mask the path of the waves, and so you should hoist the reflector at some high point on the boat – on the masthead, the backstay or on a flag halyard near the spreaders.

Left, a radar reflector about to be hoisted. A steadying line has been fixed to the bottom of it, and will be secured when the reflector is hoisted to the correct height.

NAVIGATION CONCEPTS

On any boat, large or small, for even the shortest of trips, there must be at least one person on board able to pilot or navigate the boat safely to its destination. In most small cruising boats, the skipper often takes on the job of navigator as well, which is not ideal, since there are times when both skills are needed simultaneously (as when approaching or leaving harbor, for example). It is a great help if there is another experienced sailor on board, and the skipper would be well advised to delegate one or other of the tasks to him or her.

The type of navigation skills needed will vary with the type of passage undertaken, and the nature of the waters sailed in. For a passage, or a portion of one, sailed in sight of land, pilotage skills, (or "eyeball" navigation as it is sometimes called) are needed. The most frequent need for such skills is when entering or leaving harbor. When on passage, out of sight of land occasionally, coastal navigation techniques and equipment are needed, so that a record can be kept of the boat's position. You will need basic chart skills for plotting a course, and for allowing for the effects of tidal streams. You also need to be able to fix your position using a compass and radio direction-finder.

The requirements for offshore sailing are very similar, but the navigator can expect to be out of sight of land for longer periods, and must be capable of using the coastal skills for longer periods, at night, in heavy weather or in fog, and must be completely confident of his abilities. No particularly sophisticated equipment is needed, although there is plenty available.

Once you are a long way from land, the pressure on the navigator is eased. Position fixing once a day is the norm, and it doesn't need to very accurate – a fix within ten miles may do – whereas, when coastal sailing, you may have to be accurate to within one tenth of a mile. Although the equipment needed differs slightly according to the type of cruising you are involved in, only simple and straightforward equipment and instruments are needed, although many people enjoy installing a diverse range of electronic gadgets. Many of them are good, saving time and laborious calculations. However, you must have the basic skills since the instruments could easily break down. The list below suggests which equipment should be carried and which is optional for the different types of cruising.

Pilotage
Essential: log book; binoculars; radio receiver (ordinary transistor); charts; tide tables and charts; pilot books; nautical almanac; plotting instruments – dividers, compasses, ruler, plotting instrument/parallel rulers, pencils, eraser; hand-bearing compass, steering compass; leadline; log, or distance recorder.
Optional: echo-sounder;

Coastal sailing
Essential: as for pilotage
Optional: VHF; radio direction-finding equipment; sextant.

Offshore sailing
Essential: as for pilotage plus single sideband (SSB) radio receiver.
Optional: satellite navigation equipment; Loran; Omega; automatic radio direction-finding equipment; computer navigation system linked to various inputs.

Navigation area on a medium-sized cruiser

NIGHT SAILING

Sailing at night is a normal part of any passage of more than 12 hours or so, yet many cruising sailors avoid doing so if they possibly can. Their reluctance is understandable but their apprehensions are unfounded – night sailing is not difficult and is, in fact, usually rather rewarding. Like most aspects of sailing, particular skills and techniques are needed which have to be learned and practiced. But, once acquired, they make night sailing a natural part of any cruise.

The first time you try night sailing, you should have someone on board who is experienced at it; it will help to reduce any anxiety you may feel. Your crew must be familiar enough with the boat's equipment to be able to handle it at night, and you should organize handling and stowing systems to make their task easier. Before it gets dark, try to do any jobs that you may have to do later, and consider whether any sail changes may be necessary. You could keep a smaller headsail ready for hoisting on deck in case the wind strength increases.

A watch system (see page 29) will be needed, and all crew members must have adequate rest periods. The navigator must make preparations in advance, including a list of any navigation lights that may be seen on passage, so that his work, and the crew's, is reduced during the night. No-one should go on deck unless wearing and using a harness. The navigation lights must be switched on and checked before it gets dark.

Although the boat's behavior doesn't alter at night, your impression of it, and of the conditions, will alter. It often feels rougher at night, and some people are nervous or become disorientated. Light, especially any white light, must be avoided when working on deck or steering. After some time – about 20 minutes – your eyes adjust to the dark but if a white light is used, your night vision will be seriously impaired for some time. Only a dim light or a red one should be used, both above and below decks. Although the helmsman depends largely on the compass for steering, he mustn't stare at it constantly or he will get eye-strain. The stars or moon can be used as a reference point for steering, and the compass used occasionally to check the course. The compass light should be adjusted so that it is not too bright, impairing night vision.

Judging distances at night is difficult and you must be careful not to let your imagination take charge. Normally there should be two people on watch at night, so the likelihood of both of them becoming confused or disoriented is reduced. If you, as skipper or navigator, are going off-watch, brief the crew carefully as to what to look out for and when to wake you, if anything untoward occurs. If they call you needlessly, don't lose your temper with them – they may well fail to wake you in a real emergency in future. As skipper, you must make sure you get plenty of rest. The most common mistake made by inexperienced ones is to try to do too much, with the result that they become exhausted and inefficient, ruining the cruise for all concerned.

Working on deck at dusk in the "Wight by Night" race

NAVIGATION LIGHTS

A vessel is obliged to use navigation lights at night or in poor visibility. There is an internationally agreed system of lights for all vessels, and by law you must display the appropriate ones for your boat. You also need to know how to recognize boats by their light combinations which indicate not only whether the vessel is under sail or power, for example, but its approximate size and the nature of its business. Since you are unlikely to be able to carry all the different combinations of light in your head, you should have a reference book readily available on board which gives you the full list of light combinations. As a crew member on watch, you will have to be able to report all the shipping lights to the skipper, especially if a series of bearings indicate that a vessel may be on a collision course with your own. It is up to the navigator to know the buoyage lights that will be seen during the passage and to inform the crew which ones to look out for.

The basic light arrangements for sailing and power boats are shown below: they consist of a white stern light, a red, port-side light and a green, starboard-side light. If the boat is under power it must show a white masthead light, or two if it is a large vessel. The regulations are very specific about the angle through which each light can be seen, and the ones on your boat must conform to the rules. As it is quite easy for them to move out of alignment, they should be checked periodically for accuracy. Although small sailing boats under 7m (23ft) need carry only a simple white torch and a small boat under 7m (23ft) travelling under power at less than 7 knots needs only show an all-round white light, any boat, no matter how small, would be well advised to show the full lights, for safety's sake.

You should, however, always carry a powerful torch and white flares on board (see page 144) for emergencies.

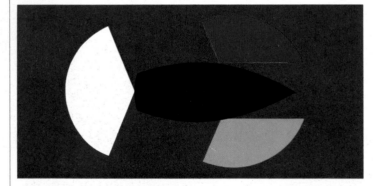

Left, sailing boats over 7m (23ft) must show a white stern light covering a 135° arc (67½° each way from dead astern) and red and green side lights covering an arc of 112.5° from dead ahead to just abaft the beam.

Below left, a power boat has to carry a white masthead light shown forwards with an arc of 225°, in addition to side and stern lights, although a boat under 20m (66ft), under power or sail, may combine the side lights.

Below, a small boat under 12m (39ft), unless it is under power, is allowed to combine the white stern light and the red and green port and starboard lights into one masthead unit, covering the same arcs.

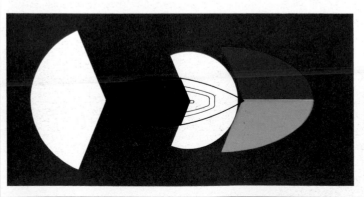

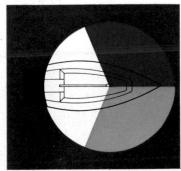

Right, a boat over 50m (164ft) under power must show a second white masthead light, shining in the same arc as the other masthead light, but positioned higher up and farther aft.

Above, any vessel aground must show an all-round white masthead light and two red all-round lights. Vessels over 50m (164ft) must show a second all-round white light lower down and farther aft.

Right, a boat at anchor must show an all round white masthead light and larger vessels over 50m (164ft) must show an additional all-round white light lower down and farther aft than the masthead light.

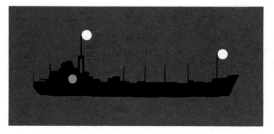

Above, a vessel constrained by her draught and restricted in her ability to maneuver must show three all-round red lights in additional to normal steaming lights.

Right, a vessel fishing but not trawling must show all-round red over white lights, but no masthead lights. If the gear extends more than 150m (492ft) an all-round white light is shown on the appropriate side.

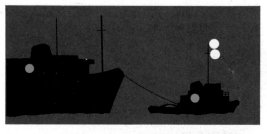

Above, with a tug and tow under 200m (656ft) the tug must show two all-round white lights, normal side and stern lights and a yellow stern light. The towed boat must show side and stern lights but no masthead lights.

Right, a pilot vessel on duty and under way must show all-round white over red lights, in addition to normal side lights and stern light.

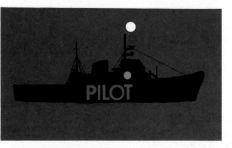

Above, a vessel of under 50m (164ft), trawling, must show an all-round green light over an all-round white light, and the usual side lights.

Right, a vessel limited in her ability to maneuver owing to her work should show red, white and red all-round lights as well as the usual masthead and side lights.

RULES OF THE ROAD

As with driving a car on highways, there are certain rules of the sea which have to be understood and obeyed by all, if collisions are to be avoided. As far as sailing is concerned, these rules are governed by international regulations and apply to all sizes of craft using both the high seas and other connected water. The rules currently in use are known as the International Regulations for the Prevention of Collisions at Sea and came into force in 1977, replacing the previous set of rules which were laid down in 1960.

Although a skipper of a larger commercial boat is likely to have received a thorough grounding in the rules and regulations, there is an equal onus on the skipper of a small boat. In the event of either of them breaking the rules, they would both be equally liable under the law, and prosecution could ensue. As with other matters, ignorance is no defence under the law, and it is your job as a boat skipper to familiarize yourself with the existing rules. In addition to the international regulations, there are often different rules for estuaries, rivers, lakes and harbors. You will need to keep a copy of the regulations aboard for handy reference.

Courses of action

If you are skippering a boat in a busy shipping channel you must keep a regular look-out. On most small and medium-sized cruisers, the crew is often short-handed and inexperienced. As skipper, you will need to know whether any boat sighted is on a collision course, but your crew may lack the experience to be able to tell you. The best solution is to ask the crew to give you details of any vessels sighted using the clock notation system, right. Once the vessel has been sighted, you need to establish whether there is a risk of collision by taking a series of bearings on the other vessel, ideally using a hand-bearing compass. If the bearings change significantly and steadily in the same direction (either increasing or decreasing), there is no danger of collision, but if they remain constant, the risk of collision exists. If you have no hand-bearing compass, simply line up the sighted vessel on a fixed object on your boat, such as a stanchion. If the vessel stays in line with you and the object, you are on a collision course. If the other vessel moves ahead in relation to the stanchion (provided, of course, you have not moved or altered your own sight-line) then it should cross your bows. If it appears to move behind the stanchion, then it will pass astern of you. If the ship is a large one take clearing bearings on both its bow and stern.

If you are on a collision course, you have

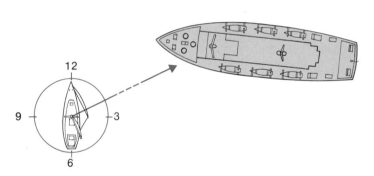

two choices. You can either stand by your rights (if you have right of way, as indicated in the rule book) or you can give way, and alter course yourself. Most small boat skippers prefer to take the latter course just in case the larger boat has not noticed them. If you do alter course, make the change substantial enough for the larger boat to be aware of your intentions. You may calculate, on your bearings, that your boat will pass just ahead of the other vessel. If it is a large commercial vessel, you might be safer to alter course to pass astern of him, just in case the wind drops or some other factors intervene which would slow your speed and put you back on a collision course. If you alter course to go astern, make sure your new course is consistent so as not to confuse the skipper of the other vessel. Continue to keep an eye on any large vessel after it has passed.

The large ship, above, would be described to the skipper of the sailboat as a "large ship at two o'clock, moving from right to left". (In practice the vessels would be considerably farther apart when sighted!)

Sound signals

Boats make their steering intentions clear to other vessels by using sound signals. The same equipment is used as for fog signals (see page 126). The International Regulations for the Prevention of Collisions at Sea lay down the rule that when vessels under power are in sight of one another, and one of them wishes to alter course or maneuver, it must indicate its intentions by the use of whistle signals (below). At night, an all-round white light can be flashed for the appropriate number of times, as well as using the whistle signal. If a vessel approaches a blind bend, or an obstruction in a channel or fairway, it should give a prolonged blast on the whistle, which is answered by a similar blast from any approaching vessel out of sight. If a vessel wishes to overtake another in a narrow channel or fairway, it must indicate its intentions, as shown below.

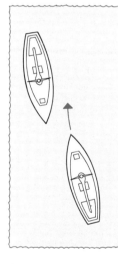 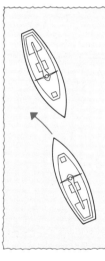 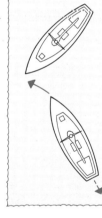

One short blast
Signal for vessel which intends to alter course to starboard

Two short blasts
Signal for vessel which intends to alter course to port

Three short blasts
Signal for vessel which has its engine in reverse

▬ ▬ •

Two long blasts, one short blast
Signal for vessel wishing to pass another vessel to starboard in a narrow channel

▬ • ▬ •

One long blast, one short blast, one long blast, one short blast
Signal for leading vessel which agrees to being overtaken

▬ ▬ • •

Two long blasts and two short blasts
Signal for vessel wishing to pass to port in a narrow channel

• • • • •

Five short blasts
Signal for vessel which wishes to indicate that another vessel's intentions are not clear

Daylight shapes

If special circumstances apply to any vessel which may demand avoiding action by another vessel, then daylight shapes are carried. They are normally of metal or plastic, and are attached where they can be most easily seen by an approaching vessel. At night, lights are shown instead (see pages 130–31).

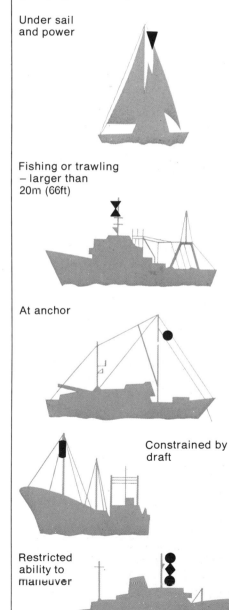

Under sail and power

Fishing or trawling – larger than 20m (66ft)

At anchor

Constrained by draft

Restricted ability to maneuver

Steering rules

The regulations lay down which vessel may hold its course, and which vessel has to give way in any situation. The three fundamental rules governing sailing craft alone are shown below, as are some of the more common rules governing other types of craft. You must refer to the full regulations for a complete guide to the rules. Since the regulations are determined to a large extent by the type and nature of the craft, you must be able to identify them. This is sometimes helped by daylight shapes (see page 133) which are carried for identification purposes, and by lights at night (see pages 130–31).

In areas of dense traffic, you will find that schemes exist to separate the vessels. Through traffic is usually separated from local traffic, and split into two streams travelling in opposite directions. There is a no go zone, known as the separation lane, between the traffic lanes which boats cannot enter except to cross it. Local traffic keeps out of the central, through-traffic area and uses the inshore zones. Any vessel entering a traffic through-lane should do so at a shallow angle (as if joining a motorway). If you have to cross a traffic through-zone, do so at right angles to the flow of traffic, and take care not to cross in front of any passing boats. Only vessels fishing, crossing over lanes, or in a state of emergency, can enter the separation zone.

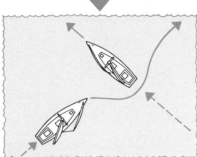

Opposite tack rule
When two boats are on opposite tacks, the port tack boat must keep clear of the starboard tack one.

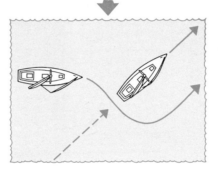

Overtaking rule
When both boats are on the same tack, the overtaking boat must keep clear of the slower boat.

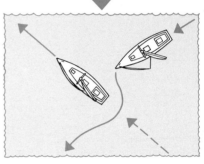

Windward rule
When both boats are on the same tack the windward boat must keep clear of the leeward one.

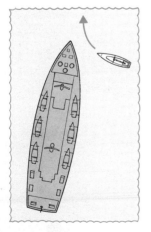

All vessels, except those not under command or restricted in ability to maneuver, must avoid impeding a vessel constrained by its draft.

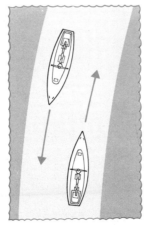

In a narrow channel or fairway, vessels must keep as close to the starboard side of the channel as possible.

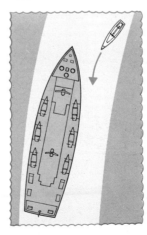

A vessel of less than 20m (66ft) or a sailing vessel must keep clear of vessels which can navigate safely only within a channel or fairway.

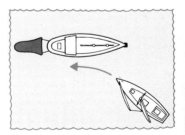

A vessel fishing or trawling (but not using trolling lines) in open water has the right of way except over a vessel not under command or with restricted maneuverability.

Right, just the type of situation to avoid, unless you have a very clear understanding of the rules of the road!

SAFETY ON BOARD

Everyone who sails knows that there is an element of danger involved and many would argue that this awareness is an integral part of the enjoyment of sailing. There is, however, a great onus of responsibility on the part of the skipper not to court unnecessary danger, and to make sure that every reasonable precaution is taken to prevent accidents occurring. Unfortunately, there are a large number of sailors who fail to appreciate the possible dangers, and therefore take inadequate precautions. Having had a few trips in good weather, they thoughtlessly take a boat into unfamiliar waters, with little knowledge of navigation or of weather, and without carrying any essential safety equipment on board.

The range of equipment you carry on board your boat will depend on its type, the size of the crew and the nature of the waters you are sailing in. Most countries lay down a recommended basic safety equipment list for pleasure boats. In the United States, the Coast Guard requires certain safety equipment, for crew and vessel; the US Power Squadron and other organizations publish recommended equipment. The checklist below shows the minimum you need.

You must know how to use the equipment you have on board, and when to use it. All the boat's equipment should be checked regularly for wear and tear, and that includes personal equipment such as lifejackets and harnesses as well as the fixed equipment. Every crew member on board should know the emergency drills, and as skipper you should rehearse the man overboard drill with them as well, on the assumption that it could be you who goes overboard.

From a more general point of view, you need to know the limitations of your crew. If you set sail with a relatively inexperienced crew, make sure you don't ask too much of them when they are tired. Carry out some simple tests at the beginning of the voyage to assess their skills and their likely reactions to emergencies. If you do run into trouble, remember that others will be involved – the Coast Guard Auxiliary, even the Navy or Air Force may be called out to help you. Don't put their lives at risk unnecessarily.

Err on the side of caution in your passage plans and try to anticipate likely problems, as well as dealing with them as they occur. Always pay attention to the weather forecasts, and don't set out if you have reason to believe the weather may deteriorate to the point where you would be unable to cope.

Safety equipment
Before setting off you must always check that you have certain items of equipment aboard, in addition to your clothes, personal possessions and sleeping gear, and water and fuel. Even if you only plan to be sailing for a few hours, you should not take the risk of being stranded out at sea without provisions and equipment, in case of an unexpected delay or failure of any part of the boat. The basic items of equipment are listed here.

- Safety harnesses
- Lifejackets or buoyancy aids.
- Life raft
- 12 assorted flares
- Fog horn

- Liferings with lights and drogues
- Dan buoy
- Drogue
- 3 fire extinguishers and 1 fire blanket

- First aid kit
- Waterproof flashlights with spare batteries and bulbs
- Radio
- Binoculars
- Spare cooking fuel
- Spare winch handle
- Spare bilge pump handle
- Spare navigation light bulbs
- Navigation instruments

- Tide tables and other reference books
- Charts
- Log book
- Plastic bucket and lanyard
- Spare lines
- Emergency supply of tinned and dried food
- Water in a separate container
- Emergency repair equipment (see page 142)

Fire prevention

Fire is one of the most serious risks on board a cruiser and it is essential to take every precaution to prevent it. Proper maintenance of the engine, stove and electrical equipment is the best way of reducing accidents caused by fire.

In the engine, fire can start as a result of fuel vapor being ignited by a spark from the starter motor, for example. Fuel pipes should be checked regularly for wear. Lining the engine compartment with a fire-retarding material, and fitting a fresh air blower and automatic fire extinguisher into the engine compartment, will also help to make your boat safer. It is important to follow a proper refuelling procedure. Always stop the engine and turn off the fuel supply to the engine first. Turn off all electrical and gas appliances and keep the companionway closed. Before restarting the engine, check that the filler cap has been securely replaced and clean up any fuel which may have been spilled. If you carry extra fuel in separate containers, these must be specially designed for the purpose and stowed on deck away from the engine and galley.

In a galley equipped with propane, the greatest danger is from a leak, as the gas collects in the bilges and may explode. A "gas sniffer" will alert you to a dangerous build up of gas. The stove mountings and gas pipes should be examined for signs of deterioration from time to time. Make sure that your crew always observe the drill of turning the gas off at the bottle (to allow the remaining gas in the pipe to burn off) before turning the knob at the stove. Always remember to turn off the gas if you leave the stove unattended. If you are going to leave the boat for any length of time, disconnect the bottle. In order to make sure that no gas or fuel vapour is allowed to accumulate in the bilges, it is a good idea to see that they are pumped out every day when the boat is in use. With alcohol stoves, the greatest danger is from overpriming and from letting the flame blow out when the alcohol is under pressure. Be sure your cook knows how to work the stove.

If a fire does break out, it is important to be calm and try to identify the source of the fire and then use the appropriate fire extinguisher (below) to put it out. It is helpful if you can reduce draft around the area of the fire to deprive it of oxygen. Continue to use the fire extinguisher until some time after the flames have gone out as there is always a risk of a fire restarting. If you are unable to control the spread of the fire, you should prepare lifejackets, flares and the liferaft, in case you have to abandon ship.

Fire-fighting equipment

Your boat should carry a variety of fire extinguishers to deal with different sorts of fire. Those that you choose should always be of good quality and you must be careful to have them checked periodically. Two different fire extinguishers are illustrated, right. The most common is the dry powder extinguisher. It is suitable for use on all types of fire. A foam fire extinguisher is particularly effective for fighting fires caused by fuel oil or cooking fat. However, this type should not be used on electrical fires and, if carried, should be supplemented by the dry powder type or a third extinguisher of the carbon dioxide type. These are mainly used for tackling fire in engines and electrical systems. A fire blanket is an important fire fighting aid which should always be kept close to hand in the galley. Using the blanket, a fire in a pan on the stove can be quickly smothered.

Fire blanket

Dry powder extinguisher   Foam extinguisher

MECHANICAL PROBLEMS

One of the greatest differences between a modern cruiser and one of, say, twenty years ago is the amount and complexity of ancillary equipment the modern boat carries. Nowadays engines are considered to be essential but a few decades ago many boats sailed without one.

Owners today expect their boat engine to be as reliable as that of their car. They want it to be powerful and yet quiet enough to run for extended periods without causing annoyance.

The quantity of ancillary electrical equipment has increased dramatically over a very short space of time. The vast majority of boats are expected to provide the usual home comforts as well as electrically operated navigation equipment. Most owners expect it to work as readily as it does at home, with very little maintenance, despite the fact that the surrounding salty atmosphere does it considerable damage. If you want expensive equipment in your boat and expect it to work, you will have to look after it properly otherwise failure is inevitable – usually at the most inconvenient time.

Electrical equipment

The most common form of electrical system for a small boat is the 12-volt DC (direct current) system, below, although both 24-volt DC and 120-volt AC (alternating current) systems are used. Both DC systems use batteries as their source of supply, and these are kept charged by an alternator on the main engine. They can also be charged by a separate generating unit, which does the job without the engine having to be run. Ideally, you should have a separate battery for starting the engine, so that if your domestic supply runs out you can still start your engine to recharge it. Whatever system you have it must be correctly wired with a bonding system that grounds any current that builds up in a metal fitting. All large metal parts should be connected via a heavy-duty copper wire to a bonding place or anode fixed on the underwater part of the hull so that any electrical build-up can be discharged. All parts of the system must be accessible. The most common problem on cruising boats is to have too many electrical items on board, so that the batteries cannot cope unless the engine or generator is run very often. As a guide, a cruising boat's electrical gear should stay operative for two to three days without the batteries being charged. If an item stops functioning, check to see if the supply is reaching it, then that the fuse or circuit-breaker is working, and the connections are properly made. If the connectors are dirty or damp, remove them and clean them. With navigation instruments, check that the sensor unit or aerial is connected, and that the instrument is turned on, and the control knobs working. Check any underwater sensors periodically to make sure they are not fouled. Service any electrical equipment regularly and remove any that you can at the end of the season.

DC system
A standard electrical arrangement for a medium-sized cruiser, using direct current, and an alternator to charge the battery.

Distribution panel

Junction box

Fuel tank

Bonding plate

Propeller shaft

Stern light

VHF radio

Cabin light

Chainplate

Pulpit light

Seacock

Switch

Battery

Alternator

Starter motor

Key

Live (+)

Return (−)

Bonding system

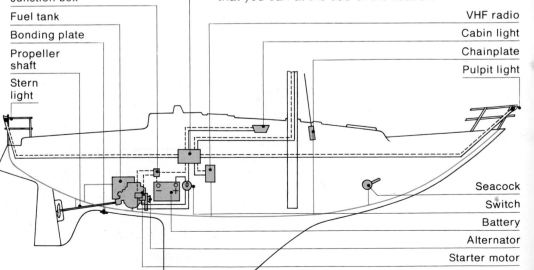

Engines

Nowadays the engine is a vital part of a cruising boat, not only for motive power but also as the primary or only source of electrical power. The majority of boats have diesel engines because they are dependable and use non-volatile fuel, but gas engines are also still used. Whichever type your boat has, it must be correctly installed and maintained. Both types need air and unpolluted fuel to function efficiently and the gas engine also requires electrical current. A diesel needs electrics only for starting, and you can often do this by hand if you have to. On all boats the fuel supply is a common source of potential trouble. Dirt and/or water can get into the fuel, either at source or on board. All tanks become contaminated eventually, either through rusting or from water which condenses in the tanks, or from leaks around the filler caps and overflow vents. To help prevent the problem, you should fit extra filters in your fuel supply, and check and clean them regularly. The tank should also be drained through the sump, normally at the end of each season, and it should have a good size inspection hole, so it can be thoroughly cleaned out. If water or dirt stops your engine, you will have to clean out the jets (on a gas engine) or the injectors.

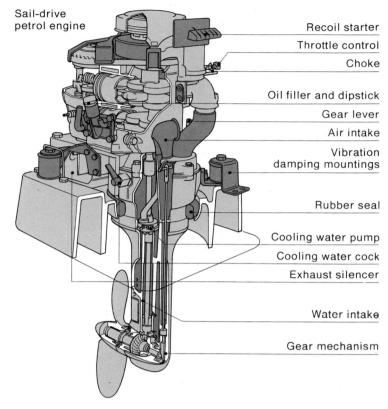

Sail-drive petrol engine

- Recoil starter
- Throttle control
- Choke
- Oil filler and dipstick
- Gear lever
- Air intake
- Vibration damping mountings
- Rubber seal
- Cooling water pump
- Cooling water cock
- Exhaust silencer
- Water intake
- Gear mechanism

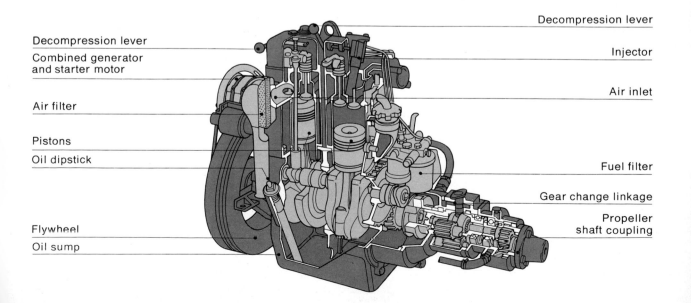

- Decompression lever
- Combined generator and starter motor
- Air filter
- Pistons
- Oil dipstick
- Flywheel
- Oil sump

- Decompression lever
- Injector
- Air inlet
- Fuel filter
- Gear change linkage
- Propeller shaft coupling

GOING AGROUND

Most skippers accidentally put their boat aground at some time or another, and suffer no ill effects other than damaged pride. However, there are times when it can be dangerous, owing to the nature of the ground or the state of the sea. If your cruising boat has a retractable keel, as some of the smaller ones do, the problem is not too difficult to solve. You can simply retract the keel a little, and float the boat off. With a fixed keel, you will either have to wait for the tide to rise to float you off, or you will have to find some way of getting the boat very quickly into deeper water. You may be able to pole a small boat out into deeper water, using an oar or a spinnaker pole, if it is not too firmly embedded. However, you would be advised to test out the nature of the seabed around the boat with a spinnaker pole or boat-hook to find out whether it is rocky and where deeper water lies. Should you have the misfortune to go aground on the top of a spring tide (known as being neaped) you may have to wait for a couple of weeks until the next really high tide before the boat can be floated off. If so, lay out anchors (see page 101) to keep the boat from drifting should it unexpectedly free itself.

Laying out an anchor, ready for the returning tide

Looking after the boat

If you have the misfortune to go aground, try to remain calm. Work out which method of freeing yourself is going to be needed and try to establish the nature of the ground under and around the boat. If you decide there is nothing you can do to help your boat to float off, make both the boat and the crew as comfortable as possible. Should the boat have gone aground heeling into deeper water (right) you must try to get it to heel over in the opposite direction (far right) to prevent it from flooding or getting damaged. To heel the boat over, move all the gear and crew weight to the opposite side of the boat. If it is already settled, you must try to pivot it around, by poling from one end or alternatively by laying out an anchor (from the dinghy in deeper water, or by wading out with it in shallow water) and then hauling on the anchor cable. Using an anchor cable can also be of vital help in getting the boat to move when the tide returns. If there is any danger of the hull being holed or torn on any jagged rocks, pad it with a folded sail or bunk cushions, attaching the padding to the boat with lines so it doesn't float off.

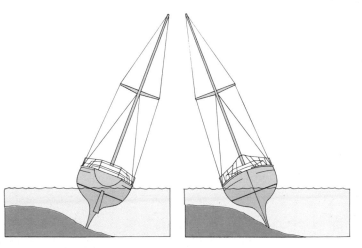

The boat, above left, has gone aground at the edge of a gulley, heeling into deeper water. It may flood when the tide returns unless it is heeled in the opposite direction

(either by moving ballast to the other side of the boat, or by pivoting it around) so that it lies against the uphill slope, (above right).

Getting off

Find out first whether the tide is rising or falling. If it is rising, with any luck you will only have to wait until the water is high enough to float the boat off. If there is any danger of the boat being pushed into shallower water as the tide rises, however, then you will have to do something to prevent it. The best solution is to lay an anchor in deeper water which you can then use to pull the boat free.

If you go aground on a falling tide, you need to work quickly to try to free the boat before the water level drops further. If you are under sail when you go aground, decide whether the sails are going to help or hinder you in your efforts to free the boat. If the latter, get them down and stowed as quickly as possible. If you go aground on the edge of a channel try to turn the bow of the boat to point into the deeper water. You may be able to do this

A stranded boat waiting for the next high tide to float it free.

by poling from the bow using a spinnaker pole or, in shallow, safe waters with a firm seabed, by going over the side (with a line attached) and pushing. The next step is to try to reduce the draught (below) so that the boat is more likely to float free. If you haven't already raised the centerboard (if you have one) make sure you now do so.

Reducing draft

The depth of draft can be altered in a number of different ways. The wind in the sails, for example, will heel the boat in a particular direction. Ballast can be shifted from one side of the boat to the other, and fore and aft, so that the point of deepest draft is altered. If you have an adventurous crew, you can persuade them to sit on the boom and then allow it to swing out over the side of the boat (having first made sure that the topping lift is strong enough!). Alternatively, you can hang a heavy weight on the end of the boom.

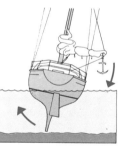

A heavy weight on the end of the boom helps to heel the boat.

If the boat is deeper aft than forward, move the weight to the bow to lift the keel free.

Using an anchor

You may have to use an anchor to pull yourself clear. Speed is important as water depth may be decreasing. Normally you use the kedge anchor and a rope rode (see page 101) and the anchor is laid as far as possible into deeper water, with the rode taken back onto the most powerful winch on the boat. As the crew grinds on the winch, spare crew members should try to heel the boat or rock it to break the keel's hold on the bottom.

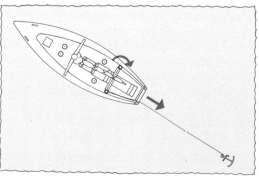

An anchor can be used to try and drag the boat off. Here the anchor rode is led around both sheet winches for extra power.

REPAIRS AT SEA

If you carry out regular maintenance and safety checks, the chances of equipment breaking will be considerably reduced. The problems commonly arise when a particular fitting or a part of the rigging breaks in heavy weather, and your difficulties will usually be increased because you will have to carry out the repairs in rough conditions. Your main objective is to make the boat seaworthy as quickly as possible, and then, if the problem is serious, to get the boat back to port, or to summon help as quickly as possible.

If a sail tears, lower it at once and rig an alternative sail, if possible. If the mainsail is damaged, you will have to sail under headsail alone, or headsail and mizzen if the boat is ketch rigged, unless you have a trysail to hoist in its place. Alternatively, you could always hoist a headsail in place of the main, fixing the head to the mainsail halyard, and the tack and clew to the boom, using it loose-footed.

You will need to make sure that you have all the repair equipment on board that may be necessary. You should take whatever engine spares the manufacturer of your particular boat engine suggests. You should also have sail repair equipment on board: a sailmaker's palm and sail needles of assorted sizes; waxed sail thread of assorted weights, spare piston hanks (if your rigging system uses them); mast slides; a marline spike and some self-adhesive sail mending tape, together with spare sailcloth.

You will need a range of general deck equipment, such as spare halyards and sheets, blocks and shackles, turnbuckles, bulldog clips and assorted screws and nails, split pins and rings. You need a small tool box with all the tools you are likely to use – such as screwdrivers, pliers, hammers, wrenches, wire cutters and saws, for example. And you need to take a range of greasing and oiling equipment, as well as insulating material and epoxy adhesive and underwater filler. Exactly what you carry depends partly on the design of the boat and partly on the amount of stowage space.

Hull damage

Should you have the misfortune to rip a hole in the hull of the boat, near or below the waterline, you need to stem the flow of water. If it is so badly damaged that the boat is in imminent danger of sinking, you should follow the procedure for abandoning ship (see page 148). The area below the waterline is particularly vulnerable to hidden obstacles beneath the water's surface. If the hole is close to the waterline mark, try to lift the damaged area out of the water by moving ballast onto the opposite side of the boat, so that the damaged part of the hull is raised up. Alternatively, you may be able to heel the boat over under sail. Your next step is to block the hole up as best you can. A small tear can be plugged with a cork, or a screwed-up cloth. In fiberglass boats, epoxy underwater filler can often be used to fill small and medium-size holes; a larger hole may have to be stuffed with a bunk cushion or sail bag, wedged in place with a fender-board or boat-hook. Once the hole is plugged, the crew must be organized to bail out the water as rapidly as possible, using the bilge pump and buckets.

If the hole is a large one, you can try to reduce the inflow by lowering a sail over the bow, having first secured lines to the clew, tack and head, and then pulling it back until it is positioned over the damaged area. Fasten the lines as tightly as possible. If you have a traditionally constructed wooden boat, you may be able to fashion a more permanent repair by plugging the hole with cloth, smeared with bedding compound and then screwing a piece of wood over the hole from inside the boat. If possible, fix another piece to the outside as well. Once you have organized some sort of temporary repair, make for the nearest port and get professional help as fast as possible.

Steering failure

Loss of steering gear requires some ingenuity on the part of the skipper. If the rudder breaks, an oar, ladder or spinnaker pole can be strongly lashed to the stern to provide some sort of temporary steering gear. In addition, the crew can try to trim the sails so that, by altering the balance between jib and mainsail, the bow of the boat can be made to move towards or away from the wind. However, in many modern designs, the boat, once rudderless, tends to swing around the keel. The solution for these types of boat is to tow a board, ladder or small bucket from the leeward quarter of the boat, which will help to pull the bow away from the wind.

Broken rigging

Occasionally, fittings may break without much warning. If a windward shroud breaks, your recourse is to put the boat immediately onto the opposite tack, to take the strain off the mast. A spare halyard already rigged can be used to take the place of the shroud, provided the shroud deck fitting is undamaged, and the halyard can be attached to it. If the fitting is broken, fasten the existing shroud to a deck eye or some other strong point. Should the headstay break, a spare halyard can be used similarly as a temporary repair. If a shroud or stay breaks near a deck fitting a new eye can be made using one or two bulldog clips. If a fitting higher up breaks, you can go aloft using a bosun's chair, right, to repair it, but this is strictly a task for the experienced.

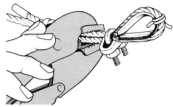

Left, a crew member ready to go aloft. The bosun's chair is shackled to a halyard, and the crew is winched up the mast. An additional safety line should also be used.

Below, a new eye made in a shroud, using a bulldog clip to fasten it in position.

Dismasting

If you maintain your mast and rigging in good condition, you are less likely to run the risk of being dismasted. Masts usually break owing to failure of the standing rigging. When the mast does break, it most commonly snaps off near the spreaders where the load on it is at its greatest, and will usually go overboard on the leeward side. You may be able to turn the boat so that the wreckage is to windward, preventing the boat from riding over the lost mast and thereby damaging the hull. Whatever you do, do not run the engine while the mast and rigging are lying in the water – the propeller will almost certainly become fouled. Your first task once the mast has broken is to try and recover the wreckage if possible or, failing that, to cut it all away with wire cutters. If sailing offshore you may well need to put up temporary replacement rigging, known as jury rigging. How this is done depends on your ingenuity, on the construction of the boat and, more particularly, on the type of mast, the amount of equipment you have on board, and on how much of the mast is left standing. With a wooden mast, the job of jury rigging is made simpler because you can screw and bolt fittings into the stump, from which temporary rigging can be attached. You

can make a temporary mast from the boom or a spinnaker pole stepped in the mast step (or lashed to the stump of the mast) on which a makeshift sail can be hoisted. Shrouds can be jury-rigged to keep the new mast in place, using spare lines and a jury rig knot (see page 154). You will have to tension the new lines using tackles. A small jib can be set in place of the mainsail.

If your boat is dismasted, you should be able to make port under a jury rig, as above.

DISTRESS SIGNALS

You must have equipment on board your boat with which to summon the rescue services or attract the attention of another boat, in an emergency. Some countries stipulate the number and type of distress signals which different craft must carry, while others leave the decision to the boat's skipper. The choice of equipment will depend on whether or not you plan to cruise offshore, but even for coastal cruising you should carry the range of flares below. They can be used in daylight or at night and have differing ranges of visibility, according to type. You must know how to use the distress signals, and where to find them. The type of distress call you make depends on the nature of the emergency. If you have a VHF set, you would normally contact the Coast Guard and give the name and position of your vessel, and the nature of the emergency.

Flares

Distress flares must only be used if there is a genuine emergency. Red flares are used at night or in daylight. Orange smoke flares also indicate an emergency, but are primarily intended for daylight use. There is a wide variety of types of flare, but the commonly available red flares can be hand-held, two-star rocket flares, or parachute flares. The latter burn for the longest time and give the greatest visibility but they are also the most expensive. In low cloud conditions, they can also be hidden if they reach high altitudes. A selection of all types should be on board, including white flares although these are not a distress signal. Their purpose is to make your presence clear to other shipping and so avoid collisions. All crew members should know where to find and how to operate all the flares carried on board. Do not keep flares after the expiry date marked on the packet has passed. They should be given to the police or the Coast Guard for disposal. To ignite a flare, follow the directions printed on the packet. Always hold the flare downwind of you and well clear of your body and any combustible items. Rocket and parachute flares should be fired downwind at an approximate angle of 45° to achieve maximum altitude.

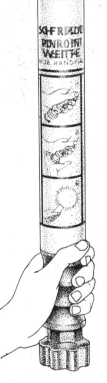

Hand-held white flare
Gives out a strong, bright white light. Use only to draw attention to yourself if collision is likely. The collision pack has four white flares.

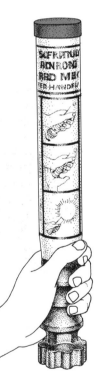

Hand-held red flare
Burns with a bright red light for one minute. Use to show exact position. Range of visibility – 4.5 km (3 miles).

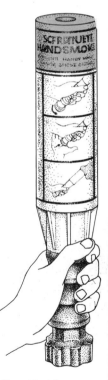

Hand-held orange smoke
Has the same use as a red hand-held flare but is used in bright daylight, when visibility is good and winds are light. It burns for about 40 seconds.

Alternative signals

There are other signals which indicate distress or the need for help. A flashlight can be used for the morse code SOS signal, right. Alternatively, you could use flags provided they are large enough to be identifiable at some distance. You need at least four code flags – the V, W, N and C. The V flag signifies that you require assistance, the W flag that you need medical assistance and the N flag flown over the C flag indicates that you are in distress and require assistance. A black square flown with a black sphere above or below it also indicates distress.

Code flag V

Code flag W

Code flag N

Code flag C

Flag and sphere

●●●——●●●
SOS signal

Red parachute rocket
Use this when a long way from help. The rocket projects a bright red flare up to 330m (1000ft) high which burns for 40 seconds.

Buoyant orange smoke
Burns for about three minutes. After ignition, drop it into the water to leeward of the boat. Useful for signalling position to an air search.

VHF radio

In most emergencies you would use your VHF set, if you had one, to make your distress call using channel 16, which is the calling and distress channel. When using the set for a distress call, switch it to channel 16 and precede the call with a "mayday" announcement, repeated three times. Then give the name of your boat, your position as a distance and bearing from a known landmark, and the nature of the emergency. The range of the transmitter is limited to the line of sight between the transmitting and receiving aerial. If you pick up a distress call on your transmitter, you should reply to the caller if no shore or ship station does so first, and then relay the message to ship or shore. Give any assistance yourself if you are close enough.

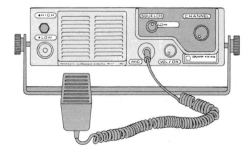

Above, a typical VHF set. Right, the hand-held call buoy which only has channel 16. It has a shorter range than the fixed set, but can be used in a dinghy or liferaft, if necessary.

RESCUING THE BOAT

In some accidents, the damage to your boat may not be sufficiently extensive to warrant abandoning ship, but of a sufficiently serious nature to prevent you proceeding under your own steam. It is the skipper's job to assess the situation, examine whatever damage has occurred, and decide whether or not the boat is still basically seaworthy, or whether the procedure for abandoning ship should be followed (see pages 148–9). In any event, it would be wise to call up the Coast Guard on the VHF transmitter, if the boat has one, or signal the problem to a passing ship, so that if anything should go wrong, help would be standing by.

If the boat has been disabled in any way further damage must be prevented from occurring. If the boat is still sufficiently seaworthy, it could presumably take a tow back to harbor. If the damage occurs when the boat is close to the harbor, it might be possible to carry out emergency measures to get the boat back to port under its own power.

Above, a disabled racing boat under tow

Salvaging

Provided the boat is not too badly damaged you may be able to limp back to port. If the hull has been damaged and the skipper decides to head for home, he should do so with all possible speed. Any emergency repairs should be started straightaway, and the boat headed for the nearest port. Use both sail and engine power, if available, to make the fastest possible passage. If the boat is taking a lot of water on board and has a diesel as opposed to a gas engine, it may be possible to keep it running by attaching a pipe to the engine air intake (to prevent this becoming waterlogged). You can use the inflatable dinghy as additional internal buoyancy, to help keep the boat afloat. If you were very close to port when the damage occurred, you could use the liferaft as well, but not if there is any likelihood that it might be needed in a hurry. If necessary, where there is a suitable stretch of beach closer than the port, head the boat for that instead. It may be possible to recover the boat with a salvage vehicle. Alternatively, you could try to get help from a larger boat, like a fishing trawler, to which your boat could be lashed to support it until salvage help can be summoned. If you radio ahead to the nearest port, the local fire brigade may send out a mobile pump to help get rid of the water.

An inflatable dinghy or liferaft can be used (below) to provide buoyancy for a sinking boat. Care must be taken to prevent it pressing against any sharp objects which could burst it. Once in port, it may be possible to tie up alongside a larger vessel such as a trawler (right). At least two heavy lines should be used and are taken right under the boat by dropping a large bight in the warps over the bow and stern and pulling them back a little towards the centre. They are then secured to the trawler.

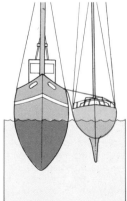

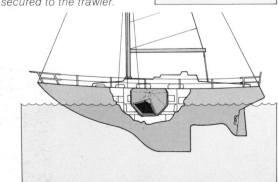

Taking a tow

If you decide to try to get a tow for your vessel, be aware that the salvaging vessel in certain circumstances can claim a fee related to the value of the vessel being towed. Any negotiations with a salvage vessel should be completed before, not after, the rescue, if at all possible. The size of the vessel offering a tow is important: large vessels do not normally travel at less than five to six knots, and your own boat may well be damaged because it will be travelling at a higher speed than it was designed for. Once you have agreed the terms of the tow with a suitable vessel, make sure that the operation is undertaken with as much regard to safety as possible. Use your own lines if you can, and protect them and the boat from chafe. The secret of successful towing is to use a long springy line and heavy chain for the tow rope, as the chain and warp together will absorb any snatching and will keep the tow line tensioned at all times, allowing

the boat to travel at a constant speed. If the rudder has been damaged, some form of jury rudder should be rigged to enable the boat to be steered to follow the towing vessel. The towed boat must always be steered in the same path as the towing boat. Extra strain will be imposed on the boat and the tow line if the boat sheers about.

When being towed, below, try to prevent the boat over-running the line. To slow the boat down it helps to trail a line with a heavy weight from the stern which prevents the boat from veering about.

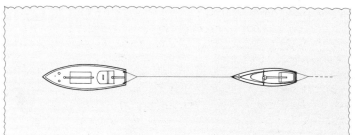

The majority of boats usually need to rig a towing bridle, which is attached to the mast and two winches. A doubled or trebled nylon rope is rigged with a towing eye on the foredeck about 60cm (2ft) aft of the bow.

The boat, right, is being towed with a strong line round the mast step. For rougher conditions, a more solid arrangement should be rigged which would minimize the risk of the line breaking under the strain.

ABANDONING SHIP

With any luck, you will never have to make the decision to abandon ship. However, you must be prepared for any eventuality, and your boat must be equally well prepared. Since disaster struck the Fastnet Race in 1979, considerable attention has been paid to the quality and type of life raft a boat should possess, and to the need to check all safety equipment regularly. It was found during the race that some boats which had been abandoned, after being disabled, were still floating quite comfortably several hours later. In coastal waters and estuaries some sailing experts consider that the dinghy is likely to serve your interests better than the life raft.

Having decided to abandon your ship for the life raft or dinghy, however, you must have adequate supplies to keep you alive until you are rescued. Most life rafts are equipped with a pack of supplies (see opposite), but a more reliable alternative is to keep a "panic bag" aboard the boat in a handy place which you can grab in an emergency. It should contain all the items shown opposite, as well as extra water, food and clothing, and should be stowed securely in a watertight container. If you manage to raise the Coast Guard or attract the attention of a passing vessel, you could be rescued directly from the boat. If you have time, protect your boat as much as possible by securing all the washboards, shutting off the seacocks and lashing down any equipment. The boat may be salvaged.

If you are rescued from the boat you could be picked up by another vessel, large or small, or by a helicopter, if the Navy has been alerted. If you are rescued by boat, it may not be easy for the other vessel to come alongside, particularly in bad weather. Your option is to use the dinghy, attaching a long warp between the dinghy and the rescue boat so that you do not lose touch. In most cases, the rescue boat crew will instruct you as to what to do. If you are being rescued by helicopter, it may not be able to hover directly over the boat for fear of becoming entangled in the mast and rigging. You will either have to get into the dinghy and move away from the boat, or jump overboard (having first donned your lifejacket). If you are the skipper of the boat, you must stay calm and, if possible, see that your crew are safe before you yourself are picked up.

The crew preparing to abandon ship: the life raft has been secured correctly on the leeward side of the boat with the canopy opening accessible to the boarding crew.

Life rafts

The life raft is the last resort in an emergency and your life may well depend upon the soundness of its construction. You must take care to purchase one which is well-made and insulated, preferably with a double floor. Most life rafts include a pack of essentials for survival (below), and you should check they are adequate. Always have the life raft checked and serviced by an approved service agent at the end of the sailing season. Make sure that the ladder of the life raft is long enough for you to board it easily.

The life raft, right, is for four people, and comes complete with the kit, below, and a boarding ladder.

The life raft pack contains all the equipment illustrated. Any extra you will have to pack yourself in a special bag to take with you.

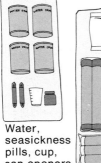

Sea anchor

First aid kit

Paddles

Fishing gear

Bailer

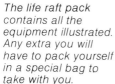

Water, seasickness pills, cup, can openers.

Survival leaflets

Quoit and line

Bellows

Flashlight batteries and bulb

Repair kit, flares, stopper, sponge, knife

Re-sealing lids

Taking to the life raft

Before abandoning ship, put on as much warm clothing as you can, and make sure that you have all the equipment you will need in the life raft, including distress signals, and as much food and water as you can carry. Untie or cut the life raft from its stowing place, and make sure that its painter is still secured to a strong point on to the boat when you throw the liferaft over the leeward side of the cruiser. The painter is designed to break under a certain load, so the life raft won't be pulled under if the boat sinks before it can be untied. The principles for boarding the life raft from the cruiser are precisely the same as for boarding a dinghy.

1 *Pick up the life raft (it will be either in a canister or a valise) and throw it over the leeward side of the boat, having first secured the static line.*

2 *Wait for the life raft to inflate fully – it should take about 30 seconds from the moment it hits the water.*

3 *When the life raft is fully inflated, the first person climbs aboard. The gear is passed down and the other crew members climb aboard. The last one unties or cuts the painter.*

KNOTS AND ROPEWORK

Rope forms a vital part of the boat's equipment and is expensive to replace. Learning how to handle rope and to look after it properly are an essential part of your seamanship skills. You will lengthen the life of your ropes if you do not allow them to chafe against sharp or abrasive objects. If they do wear in one place you can sometimes repair them by cutting out the frayed part and splicing the ends together (see page 155). Rope ends should be whipped to prevent them unravelling (see also page 155).

Over the years sailors have added to their repertoire of knots. The selection on these pages includes the most commonly used. Some are multi-purpose knots, others have a more specific task – the rolling hitch, for example, will take strain in one specific direction. Make sure you can tie them quickly and accurately – your safety may well depend on them one day.

Parts of the knot

Knotting, like sailing, has its own terminology. The bend you make in a rope when knotting it is known as the bight. The part of the rope under strain is known as the standing part.

Bight

Standing part

Figure of eight

The main purpose of this knot is to put a stopper at the end of a rope. It is easy to tie and equally easy to undo.

Types of rope

Although rope was formerly made of natural fibres, synthetics are now more commonly used. They are more hard-wearing than natural fibre, but some tend to become slippery when wet.

The actual construction of the rope is either laid – where the strands are twisted together – or braided, where they are interwoven. Mooring warps are usually of three-strand laid construction, while sheets and halyards are usually braided.

The type and thickness of the rope depends largely on its function. Although braided ropes are more durable and more pleasant to handle than the laid variety, they cannot be repaired by splicing.

Polypropylene three-strand

Nylon octoplait

Nylon eightplait

Polyester three-strand

Nylon braidline

Square knot

This knot, originally devised to tie the reefing lines of a sail, is formed from two half-hitches, tied in opposite directions. If you inadvertently tie them in the same direction, the resulting knot will jam. It is known as a "granny knot". Take care to tie the knot exactly as shown.

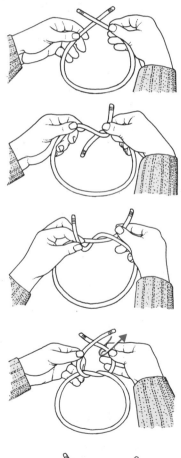

Undoing a square knot

A square knot can be quickly and easily untied by grasping one end of the knot in one hand and the standing part in the other, pulling apart to "upset" the knot and then pushing the knot off the standing part, as shown.

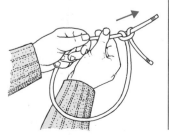

Sheet bend

Use this knot to join two ropes, in particular those of unequal thickness. To undo the knot, bend it in the center and push the bight down on the half-hitch.

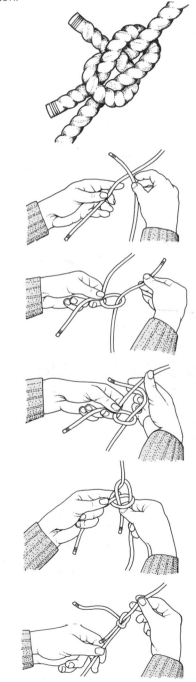

Round turn and two half-hitches

This is one of the most commonly used knots of all. It is used to tie a rope to any standing object and is easy and quick both to tie and to undo, provided there is no great strain on the rope. Two half-hitches should be sufficient to secure the rope.

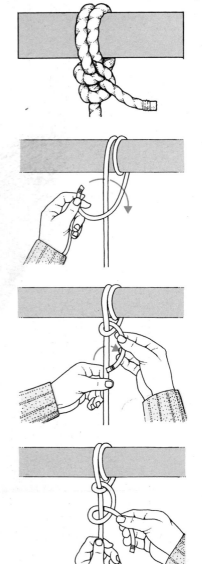

Clove hitch

Use this knot to tie small items temporarily, such as fenders, to stanchions. It holds well only when under steady strain at right angles to the standing object to which it is fixed. If there is any lateral or jerking strain, it may well come undone.

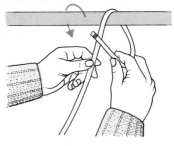

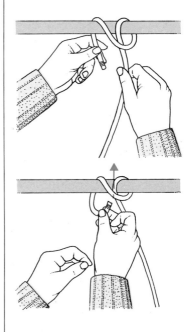

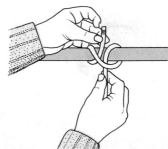

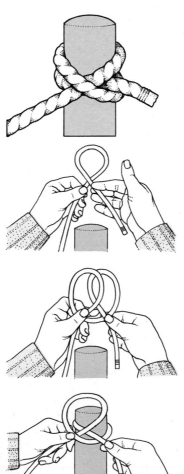

Clove hitch around a bollard
If you are tying up temporarily to a bollard, you can use the quick method below. The rope is coiled in the hand, as shown, and the loops dropped over the bollard. Use a half-hitch if you wish to secure the knot more firmly.

Bowline

This knot is used for a number of tasks. Since beginners can find it hard to tie, an easy method is shown below — there are others. Learn to tie the knot with the standing part both towards you and away from you.

Rolling hitch

This knot is useful if you wish to put strain on the knot which is parallel to the object to which it is tied — the more pressure you apply in the right direction, the tighter the knot becomes.

Becket hitch

This is a useful knot for securing a line to an eye or hook. Up to step 3 it is known as a single becket hitch. Step 4 turns it into a double becket hitch, which permits the knot to take greater strain.

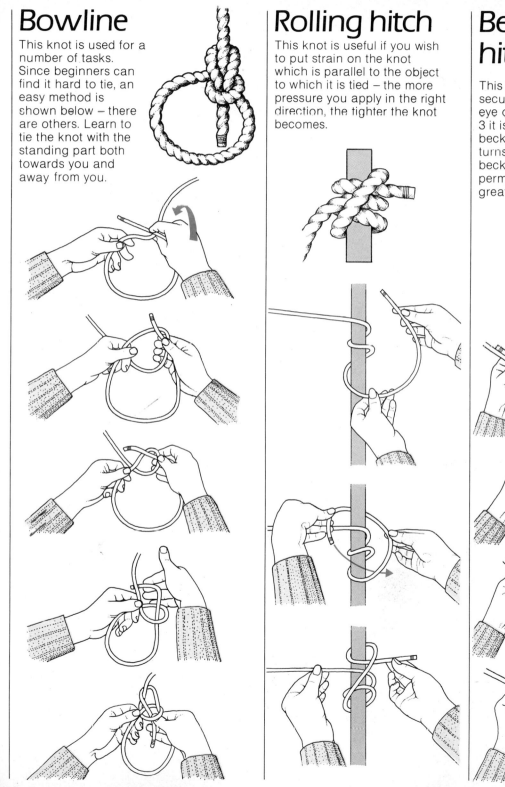

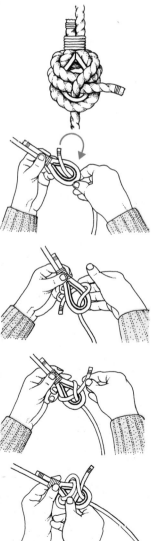

Quick-release knot

There are a number of knots which can be tied so that they can be released quickly, usually by looping over the end of the rope to tie the knot. The most commonly used is the quick-release version of the round turn and two half-hitches. You can add a further half-hitch (bottom) for a more secure knot, although it will not release quite as quickly.

1 *Make a round turn in the usual way.*

2 *Double the rope end to form a loop and lay the loop over the standing part.*

3 *Make a half-hitch with the loop around the standing part, and pull tight.*

4 *At this stage, the knot can be quickly released, even under strain, by pulling on the end of the rope.*

For greater security, a half-hitch can be made although the knot cannot be released so easily.

Jury rig knot

If your boat is dismasted, a spare spar can be rigged as a temporary mast by using a jury rig knot. It provides four loops if you tie the two loose ends with a bowline.

Whipping

To prevent ropes unravelling, they should be finished by whipping the ends with twine. Be careful to whip the rope in the opposite direction from the lay.

Finished whipping

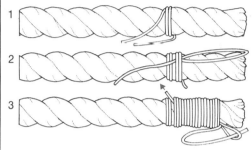

1

2

3

Splicing

Splicing is a way of joining two ropes by weaving the ends together. The short splice, below, is easy to learn but it increases the diameter of the rope and weakens it.

Finished splice

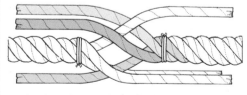

1 Bind each rope 15cm (6in) away from the end and unravel them to this point. Place the two ends together as shown.

2 Bind the loose strands of one rope to the other and remove the twine from the first rope. Start to weave in the loose strands in turn as shown above, turning the rope as you work. Continue until each strand has been threaded through at least three times. Repeat the process with the other rope and trim the ends.

Eye splice

An eye splice is used to form a fixed loop of any size in the end of a rope. It is sometimes put into the end of a mooring line, and has the advantage of being stronger than any knot.

To make the splice, you must first unlay the strands of the rope for a sufficient distance to complete five full tucks under the strands. Whip the rope to prevent the strands unravelling before you start.

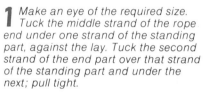

1 Make an eye of the required size. Tuck the middle strand of the rope end under one strand of the standing part, against the lay. Tuck the second strand of the end part over that strand of the standing part and under the next; pull tight.

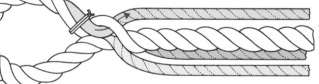

2 Turn the splice over and tuck the last full strand under the remaining strand in the rope. Pull tight again.

3 Continue tucking each strand in turn alternatively passing over and under the strands in the standing part. Pull tight after each series of tucks.

4 When you have completed five tucks in each strand, cut off the loose ends. You can taper the strands for the last two tucks to give a neater appearance.

GLOSSARY

A

Aback Said of a sail when, with its clew to windward, it is pressed back against the mast. It may occur due to a sudden change of wind or be done on purpose as when hove-to (see *Heave-to*).

A-hull A boat is a-hull when it is riding at sea with no sails set and its helm to leeward.

Anchor A heavy metal implement used to secure a vessel to the seabed.

Anti-fouling A paint compound used to protect the underwater part of a boat from the growth of marine life.

Apparent wind The wind that flows over a moving boat. The sum of the true and the created wind.

Athwartships At right angles to the fore-and-aft line of a vessel.

B

Backing a sail To push a sail out so that the wind fills it from the opposite side, and the boat slows down.

Backstay A stay fitted as standing rigging to prevent forward movement in the mast.

Bail To remove water with a bucket or other container.

Bare poles, to sail under To sail without any sails set.

Batten Light wooden or plastic strip inserted into a pocket in a sail to shape the leech.

Batten down To secure and, if necessary, tie down fittings, such as hatches, in preparation for heavy weather.

Bearing The direction of one object from another. It can be measured in degrees true or degrees magnetic.

Bend (1) To attach a sail to its spar; (2) to attach two ropes together by means of a knot.

Bermudian rig Another term for a Marconi rig.

Bight A loop in a rope.

Bilge The lower, rounded part of a vessel. A bilge pump is used to remove excess water from the bilges of the boat.

Block The nautical term for a pulley.

Bolt rope A reinforcing line along the edge of a sail.

Boom A spar which is used to extend the foot of a sail.

Boom preventer (see *Preventer*)

Boom vang Line or tackle to hold the boom down. Also called a "kicking strap".

Bosun's chair Usually a canvas bucket seat on which a person can sit and be hoisted aloft to carry out repairs.

Bow The forward end of a vessel.

Breast line A line used for tying up to a jetty, and which is led approximately at right angles to the side of the boat.

Broach The action of a boat when, running before a sea, it slews round inadvertently, broadside on to the waves.

C

Cable See *Rode*.

Carvel Form of wooden boat construction in which timber planks are laid flush over wooden ribs.

Chainplates Metal fittings on the sides of a boat, to which the shrouds are attached.

Chine The angle of a junction between two flat sides of a hull.

Chord An imaginary curved line between the luff and the leech of a sail, parallel to the foot.

Cleat A wooden or metal fastening with two arms, around which lines can be made fast.

Clew The lower aft corner of a fore-and-aft sail.

Clinker A form of hull construction in which planks are laid fore-and-aft, overlapping at the edges.

Cockpit A well in the deck where the tiller or steering wheel is located.

Companionway A ladder leading from the deck to the cabin or saloon.

Compass An instrument used to indicate direction relative to the earth's magnetic field.

Cringle A loop or eye set into the bolt rope of a sail.

Cunningham hole An eye in the luff of a sail above the tack, which allows the luff tension to be adjusted.

Cutter Single-masted boat with two headsails.

D

Dodger Canvas hood protecting a companionway from spray.

Double-ender Any boat with a pointed bow and stern.

Downhaul Tackle used for pulling down the tack and tensioning the luff of a sail.

Draft Vertical distance measured from the waterline to the lowest point of the hull.

Drogue Object towed to reduce speed.

F

Fairlead Any ring, bolt, eye or loop which guides a rope in the direction required.

Fairway Main channel down which boats should travel in restricted waters.

Fall The part of the rope that is hauled on in a tackle.

Fathom A measurement used for depth, one fathom equals six feet.

Fender A cushion of durable material inserted between a boat and some other object, to prevent direct contact or chafe.

Foot The lower edge of a sail.

Fore-and-aft In line from bow to stern; on, or parallel to, the centreline.

Forepeak A space in the bows of a vessel, right forward.

Foresail Triangular-shaped sail set forward of the mast and abaft the jib.

Forestay A stay leading from the mast to the foredeck abaft the headstay.

Freeboard The portion of a vessel's hull which is not submerged.

Freer See *Lift*.

Furl To roll a sail and secure it to its boom.

G

Gaff A spar which extends the head of a four-sided fore-and-aft mainsail.

Genoa A large headsail which extends abaft the mast.

Gimbals A system by which an object is suspended so that it remains horizontal.

Go about To turn the boat from one tack to the other.

Gooseneck The universal joint fitting on a mast to which the boom is attached.

Grabrail A hand-hold on a boat.

Ground tackle Generic term for anchoring equipment.

Gunter rig A rig in which a gaff slides up the mast to form an extension to it.

H

Halyard A rope or wire by which a sail or flag is hoisted.

Hanks Snaphooks by which sails are attached to stays.

Hard eye A reinforced wire loop.

Header A wind shift farther forward relative to the boat.

Headsail A sail set forward of the main mast.

Head sea A sea flowing in the opposite direction to that in which the boat travels.

Head-to-wind With the bow facing into the wind.

Heave-to (1) To stop the boat by backing a headsail and lashing the tiller; (2) to slow the boat by letting the sails flap on a beam reach (used for short periods only).

Holding ground Part of the seabed where the anchor digs in.

I

In irons A boat is said to be in irons when it has stopped or is moving backwards because it is pointing directly into the wind.

J

Jackline Rigged line to which safety harness can be clipped.

Jury rig A temporary replacement of any part of the boat's rigging, set up after damage or breakage.

K

Kedge (1) A small auxiliary anchor; (2) to kedge is to move a vessel by laying out the kedge and pulling on it.

Keel The fixed underwater part of a sailing boat used to prevent sideways drift and provide stability.

Ketch A two-masted, fore-and-aft rigged boat. The

forward mast is the mainmast; the shorter mizzen mast is stepped aft, forward of the rudder post.
Knot A measure of speed: one nautical mile (6060.2 feet) per hour.

L

Lacing A length of line or thin rope.
Lashing A line used for securing any movable object.
Lazy guy A guy which is not in use, that is, taking no strain.
Lead (1) A lead weight attached to the end of a line, used to ascertain the depth of water beneath a boat and the nature of the seabed; (2) the path taken by a rope, usually between a sail and a fairlead or winch.
Lee (1) The area to leeward (downwind); (2) to be "in the lee" of an object is to be sheltered by it.
Leeboards (1) Boards fixed vertically to the outside of the hull to prevent leeway; (2) boards fitted to the outside of a bunk to prevent the occupant falling out.
Leech The aftermost edge of a fore-and-aft sail; both side edges of a square sail.
Leeward Away from the wind.
Leeway The sideways movement of a boat induced by wind or wave pressure (sideslip).
Let fly To let a sheet go, thus spilling the wind from the sail.
Lifeline Safety line fitted around an open deck.
Lift A wind shift farther aft relative to the boat, which permits it to sail higher; opposite of a header.
Log Instrument used to measure the vessel's speed through the water.
Luff (1) Forward edge of a sail; (2) to luff or luff up is to sail closer to the wind so that the sails luff.
Lug (or lugsail) A four-sided sail, bent onto a yard, and slung to the mast in a fore-and-aft position.

M

Marconi rig The modern sailing rig, with a tall triangular mainsail; also

called Bermudian or jib-headed rig.
Marline spike A pointed tapering iron used for opening the strands of wire during splicing.
Mast A pole, or system of attached poles, placed vertically on a vessel, used to support the sails.
Mast step A recess in a vessel's keel into which the base of the mast is positioned.
Meter class A form of rating for a boat based on a certain measurement formula.
Mizzen (1) The aftermost mast of various rigs; (2) the fore-and-aft sail hoisted on the mizzen mast.
Molded hull One which is built up by bonding layers of veneer or by the use of a mold, as in fiberglass construction.

N

Nautical mile One 60th of a degree of latitude (a minute); slightly longer than a standard mile (6060.2 feet).
Navigation lights Lights (with different-colored sectors) required to be shown on vessels at night, to enable identification to be made.
No-go zone Area into which a boat cannot sail without tacking.

O

Offwind Any point of sailing away from the wind.
One-design Any boat built to conform to rules so that it is identical to all others in the same class.
Outhaul A rope which hauls out something, as the clew outhaul does the clew of the mainsail.

P

Pilot Sailing directions.
Pinch To sail too close to the wind.
Plot To mark courses, bearings and directions on a chart.
Points of sailing The different angles from the wind on which a boat may sail.
Port The left hand side of a vessel (when looking

forward); a boat is on "port tack" when the wind is blowing over its port side.
Preventer Additional line or tackle that is set up to prevent movement in a mast or boom. A boom preventer is a line or tackle set up to prevent an accidental jibe.
Prop walk The sideways effect the propeller has on the stern of a boat, particularly at slow speeds.
Pulpit An elevated guardrail set up at either the bow or the stern, or both. The one at the stern is often known as a pushpit.
Purchase Any tackle or manner of leverage used to raise or move some object.
Pushpit See *Pulpit*.

Q

Quarter That portion of the ship midway between the beam and the stern. "On the quarter" applies to a bearing 45° abaft the beam.
Quarter berth A bunk which runs under the side of the cockpit.

R

Race A strong, confused tide or current.
Range (1) Two fixed objects form a range when they are in line. Ranges are often used as leading marks to help guide a navigator into a harbor; (2) the difference in the depth of water between high and low tides.
Rating A method of measuring certain dimensions of yachts of different sizes and types so that they can race on a handicap basis.
Reach To sail with the wind approximately over the beam.
Reef To reduce the sail area by folding or rolling.
Reef cringles The eyes in the leech and luff of the sail through which the reef pendants are passed.
Reef points Short pieces of rope hung from each side of the sail, used to tie up the reefed portion of a sail.
Restricted class A class of boats built to fixed dimensions but with others which may vary.
Riding light An all-round white light, hoisted on the

headstay when a boat is at anchor.
Rigging Wires and ropes used to keep the mast in place and to work the sails.
Roach The curved leech of a sail.
Rode The line or chain attached to the anchor. Sometimes called "cable".
Running backstay A movable backstay.
Running rigging The generic term for sheets and halyards. The lines that hoist and trim the sails.

S

Sampson post A strong vertical post to which docking lines or the anchor rode can be secured.
Schooner A boat with two or more masts, in which the mainmast is the aftermost mast.
Scope Length of anchor rode that is paid out, or the distance it covers.
Sea anchor Any form of drogue employed as a floating anchor, and used to help a boat ride out a gale.
Seacock A valve fitted to an underwater inlet on a vessel.
Shackle An openable link used to attach lines, sheets, halyards, etc.
Shank The main shaft or leg of an anchor.
Sheet A rope attached to the clew or a sail, to allow the sail to be trimmed. When the sheets are brought in and made fast they are said to be sheeted home.
Shrouds Wires that support the mast on either side; part of the "standing rigging".
Slack tide A short period at the turn of the tide when there is no tidal flow in either direction.
Slip (1) To deliberately let go; (2) a slip line is a double line, securing the boat to an object, with both ends of the rope made fast on board.
Sloop A single-masted boat with one headsail only. It can be gaff or Marconi rigged.
Soundings Assessment of depth of water.
Spars A generic term for masts, booms, gaffs or bowsprits.
Spinnaker A lightweight three-cornered sail set flying from the mast, and controlled

INDEX

ACKNOWLEDGMENTS

Photographic Sources
(B = Bottom, C = Centre, T = Top, L = Left, R = Right)

Avon Inflatables Ltd: 149
R. R. Baxter: 120
Beken: Title, 13, 14R, 15
Alastair Black: Half title, 10, 11, 14L, 27, 46, 47, 49, 71R, 108BR, 109, 111, 113, 117, 119, 121T, 129
Bob Bond: 41B
Jack Coote: 19L
Dick Everitt: 18TR
Bob Gordon: 53
Ambrose Greenway: 146
Colin Jarman: 18BR, 19BR, 75, 114, 115B, 121B, 135
National Maritime Museum: 12
Mike Payton: 140
Sue Rawkins: 143T
RNLI: 147
Stephen Sleight: 37, 99, 128
M. A. Stock: 18L
John Watney: 17, 19TR, 20, 21, 29, 71L, 100, 103, 104, 125, 127, 143B, 148
Rodger Witt: 141
Steven Wooster: Foreword, 23, 25, 33, 35, 36, 39, 40TL, 40TR, 41, 42, 43, 44, 45, 50, 51, 52, 54, 56, 57, 58, 59, 60, 61, 63, 64, 65, 66, 67, 68, 72, 73, 74, 76, 77, 79, 80, 81, 83, 84, 86, 87, 88, 92, 93, 96, 98, 101, 107, 108BL, 108C, 110, 112, 115TL, 115TR, 115CL, 115CR, 118, 124

Dorling Kindersley would like to thank the following individuals and organizations who cooperated in the production of this book:

The staff of the National Sailing Centre, Cowes, for the use of their boats and their invaluable advice and instruction.

Gill and Paul Edden for the loan of their Contessa and for demonstrating sailing techniques, and Julian Mannering for his hard work as a crew.

Steven Wooster for taking so many of the photographs and for the origination of the design of the book, and Gillian Della Casa for her help also with the design.

Capt. O. M. Watts Ltd for permission to take photographs of their chandlery.

Illustrations by
David Ashby
David Etchell
Andrew Farmer
John Ridyard
Les Smith
Venner Artists

Typesetting by
MS Filmsetting Ltd, Frome

Reproduction by
Reprocolor Llovet, S.A.,
Barcelona

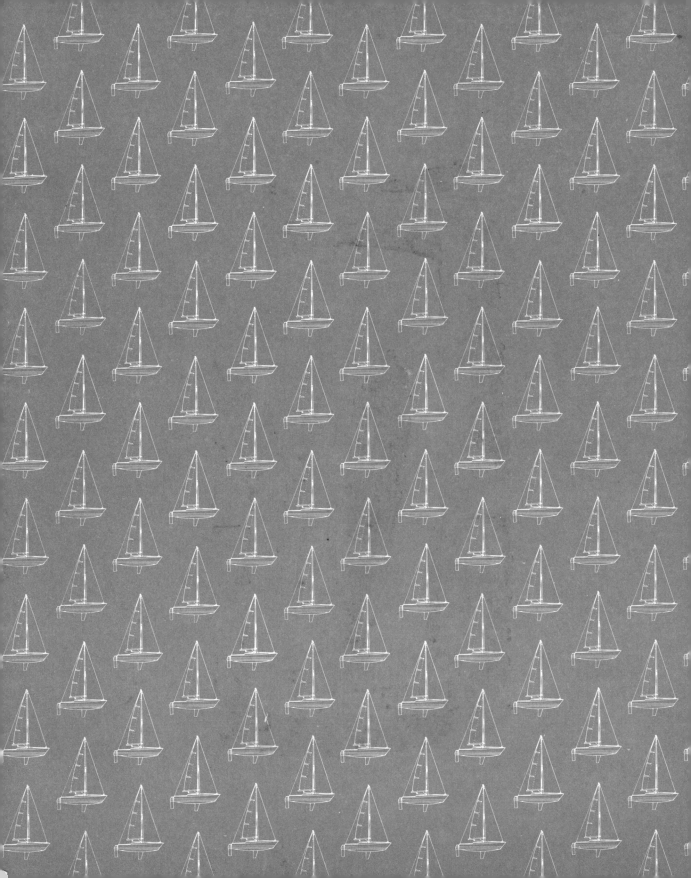